Eric Liddell

God's Athlete

Catherine M. Swift

MarshallPickering

Marshall Pickering is an Imprint of
HarperCollins*Religious*
Part of HarperCollins*Publishers*
77–85 Fulham Palace Road,
Hammersmith, London W6 8JB

First published in Great Britain
in 1986 by Marshall Pickering

4   6   8   10   9   7   5

A catalogue record for this book is
available from the British Library

ISBN 0 551 01354 0

Set in Plantin

Printed in Great Britain by
HarperCollinsManufacturing Glasgow

Contents

1: China

Being a vast, colourful land of beauty and mystery, China has always held a fascination for the rest of the world. Yet, in the past, few visitors ever ventured there and those who did were rarely welcomed by its yellow-skinned, almond-eyed people.

As it is surrounded by dense forest, arid desert and high mountains, with the Pacific Ocean to the east, it is perhaps understandable why China received so few visitors from the outside world. Still, from the beginning of time, China was constantly being invaded and overcome by its nearest neighbours; Manchuria, Tibet, Turkestan and Mongolia. Each conqueror would set up a new dynasty and when Ch'ing, the last one, drew to a close in 1912, there had been no less than twenty ruling dynasties (families).

In an effort to keep these invaders from China's territory, the Great Wall was built in the third century BC. But this only made the vast nation even more isolated from the rest of the world and foreign traders.

China was always a self-sufficient country with its own foodstuffs, merchandise, fuel and minerals so it may seem unreasonable that the Chinese should want trade with anyone outside their own borders. However, there was a very good reason for it.

In the far-distant past, as in the rest of the world, bartering had been the normal trading method in China until it was realised that coins made from precious metals were more durable than, say, a payment of livestock or food. China was the first country in the world to make coins. They were produced in various sizes, each size carrying a different value and were made of silver, one of the few metals China could not produce. It would have been of no use to trade in one which was abundant because it would then not have as much value. China needed an export trade.

The goods most popular with foreign merchants in exchange for the treasured metal were tea, cotton, porcelain, rice, silk and jade. But before long, unscrupulous dealers began to pay with something which cost far less than silver. They began to import opium into the country and soon most of China's exports were being traded for the evil drug rather than for the silver she needed so much.

People in high places fell under its corrupt influence and soon, China was not only being exploited by foreign merchants, but also by its own government officials – even by the Emperor's court itself.

With all of the wealth finding its way into the wrong hands, the economy began to fail and China was heading for poverty.

When the Great Wall had failed to keep out her invaders, China had, long ago, invaded their lands and taken them over along with their people. This meant there were *five hundred million* mouths to feed and with general neglect throughout the land, famines were occurring regularly. In one of them, *ten million* people died.

By the nineteenth century, throughout the western world, due to education, new discoveries and inventions, countries were being modernised. But Chinese rulers were doing nothing for their people and the peasants' anger was whipped up. Rebellions broke out everywhere and more millions died.

8

Russia, Japan, Britain and France had always wanted to establish diplomatic relations with China. Now, because of the wicked opium dealers and China's selfish rulers, the country was in a hopeless state and quite unable to defend itself so all those countries took advantage of her. They made war and soon these modern day invaders occupied large areas of China, including Peking, the capital.

Eventually a conditional peace was made between Britain and China. In 1858, a treaty was signed at Tientsin, a city in the north east. The terms were that more ports must be opened to foreign traders. The valuable trading port of Hong Kong was to become a British Colony. China was to accept foreign ambassadors and grant concessions – areas of her country, mostly in towns and cities, where foreigners would live under their own laws and government. Some Chinese would be permitted to live inside the concessions but they would be ruled by that country's laws. Furthermore, Christian missionaries must be allowed to live in and freely move about the entire country, teaching their beliefs to the Chinese who already had several gods of their own.

All this resulted in many Chinese people hating everyone and anything from outside their own country and culture.

They thought westerners were rude and uncivilised with their loud voices. They never bowed nor constantly smiled at each other and they ate their food in great mouthfuls using metal knives and forks instead of the dainty portions the Chinese ate with bamboo or ivory chopsticks.

But for every Chinese who hated foreigners, there was another who hated their own ruler even more.

When the Emperor, Hsien Peng, had died in 1861, he left his five-year-old son to follow him. Of course no child of that age could actually rule a nation and, in such cases, the country is ruled by a Regency – a group of people sharing the responsibility for running the country until the rightful ruler is able. The Emperor's widow, Tz'u Hsi was to be one of this group but as she disapproved of the other three Regents, she had them murdered and took charge herself to rule China the way she wanted.

There is a part of Peking called the Forbidden City. This is really a cluster of palaces built close to each other. In one of them Tz'u Hsi sat on the turquoise and jade encrusted gold Dragon Throne. She wore the most beautiful robes of jewel-encrusted satin, heavily embroidered with gold thread and her fingernails grew several inches long to show that she never did any work.

Thousands of servants ministered to her every whim and when she wanted to move from room to room—the Forbidden City palaces have 9999 rooms—she was carried on a litter because her feet were never to touch the floor. Gongs and bells warned of her approach giving others time to get out of the procession's path, or else! Stone and bronze lions and unicorns glared down threateningly on everyone.

Some of the palaces were situated on islands in lakes—right there in the middle of Peking—and if the Empress fancied visiting one of them or going for a picnic to the lake, a matter of minutes away, dozens of servants accompanied her.

They carried several changes of clothes, umbrellas, parasols and fans in case she got too warm, too cold, the sun was too hot or it rained. Doctors with medicine and pills went along in case she fell ill on the journey. Food and drink by the case full went in case she felt hungry or thirsty.

She had her own theatre in one of the palaces but it was no honour to entertain her. If she wasn't thoroughly pleased with a performance, the entertainer was severely punished.

When the young Emperor, T'ung Chih, eventually came to the throne, to his mother's great disappointment, he was very impressed with the modern ways of the western world. Determined to lift China out of centuries of despair, he encouraged the young people to travel abroad. They would learn and adopt new ideas from other countries. Then T'ung Chih built a university in Peking where returning students could educate even more of the youth of China.

His mother was outraged and felt no heartbreak when her son died in 1875 at the age of nineteen, leaving a pregnant widow.

Tz'u Hsi was so worried her grandson would be like his father she hastily arranged to have her sister's son crowned Emperor before her own grandson could be born. Her nephew was another young child and again his aunt became Regent until he came of age.

He ascended the Dragon throne in 1889 but to his aunt's horror he turned out to be exactly the same sort of ruler as his cousin had been. With the intention of improving China's economy, he allowed foreign industrialists to build railways while others opened tin and iron mines.

Of course, Tz'u Hsi saw her nephew as a traitor to old ways and beliefs, so she plotted against him.

China abounded with illegal secret societies at that time. The most evil of these was the White Lotus Society. There was an offshoot of this Society which was even more criminal and evil than the main body. They called themselves the Ho Chuan—Fists of Righteous Harmony but known in the West as the Boxers. This was because of their training methods which included punching hard objects to make their fists as strong as steel.

The Boxers were filled with hate for all foreign things and people and their sole aim was to rid China of anything that didn't belong there. They were so harsh in their ways that if a Boxer broke a society rule, not only was he put to death but also his entire family with him.

Although Tz'u Hsi knew these secret societies were illegal, she set about giving this particular one all the help she could.

At the time of all this upheaval in China, on the other side of the world – about 5,000 miles away – in a small Scottish village near Loch Lomond, there lived a grocer and his family.

The Liddell family paid scant attention to what was going on in that strange, oriental land across the seas. Their chief occupation was bringing up their family, selling food to the villagers of Drymen and, with a little white pony and cart, running a transport service for passengers and mail to and from the railway station.

They were pleasant, hard-working, neighbourly people if rather quiet and reserved. The one time their reservation was dropped was whenever they attended religious meetings in the village square and sang out loudly and proudly.

Their neighbours were always surprised at this undisguised display of devotion. Some were mildly amused or embarrassed by it, others were quite critical.

The Liddells' son, James, was apprenticed to a draper in Stirling city, a few miles away from his native village. James was content with his choice of career until one year when he went on holiday and met William Blair, a Congregational Church minister. Coming from a strong Methodist family himself, James soon formed a close friendship with the Reverend Blair. The two discussed the church and its work and, in particular, the work of its missionaries abroad.

After that holiday, James was really unsettled. It was as though something new had awakened in him which had nothing to do with the drapery business. He was being called into the church and the call was coming from a far-off

12

land. But where? No name came to him but he was sure God had some mission planned for him.

Mary Reddin, a young girl from Berwickshire, a border county lying between England and Scotland was working as a nurse in a Glasgow hospital. She had recently been ill and some friends invited her to their home in Stirling for a short convalescent holiday. While she was there, the time came around for the annual Sunday School picnic and Mary went with her friends.

Young James Liddell attended that picnic too and they were introduced to each other. As neither of them belonged to the area, they felt a bit out of things with all the revelry going on among people who knew each other well. They spent the entire afternoon talking to each other with Mary explaining how she came to be there. James told her of how his outlook on life had recently changed and that he was planning to become a church minister. Mary listened carefully, nodding her head in understanding and admiration, feeling as much enthusiasm as he did about it.

In this pretty, dark-haired girl, James saw a sweet-natured, sympathetic character. In him, Mary saw a big-hearted man who was only too happy to leap up from his chair to tend to the needs of anyone there, even a stranger who was still feeling rather poorly.

During her stay in Stirling they met frequently and when Mary was back nursing in Glasgow, they wrote regularly. Before long, they realised they were very much in love and James asked her to marry him. Mary accepted at once. However, James had another question for her. Would she be willing to be, not only the wife of a minister but the wife of a missionary in foreign lands where he was sure his destiny lay? Without a moment's hesitation Mary said she would go to the ends of the earth with him.

James immediately applied for an ordination course in Glasgow and Mary stood beside his proud family and friends when they later attended his ordination in Glasgow at the Dundas Street Congregational Church.

Now, with his long hours of study behind him, they thought they would soon be married – but it was not to be – not at that time.

James was determined to take up missionary work straight away so he applied to the London Mission Society for their specialist course in working abroad.

It was 1897, the same year that the Chinese Empress, T'zu Hsi joined forces with the secret society of Boxers.

James and Mary were disappointed to be told they could not marry until he had both completed this second course and done a year's missionary work in a foreign country.

Passing his exams would not necessarily mean the Reverend James Liddell would make a good missionary. Only practical experience could decide that. As it would be very costly for the society to send Mary abroad too, James would have to prove himself worthy of his calling before she could join him.

He worked diligently to complete the London Mission Society course and pass his exams, and did so quite easily. Then, although he was a patient man, excitement mounted in him daily as he waited to hear where his official posting would be. Finally it arrived. He was being sent to Mongolia in the far north of China.

Mary was just as excited when she heard the news. Once James had a few months' work experience behind him in China, she was certain to be setting sail from her native Scotland to join the man she loved. They had not seen very much of each other during his studies because Mary had gone to work on Lewis, one of the remote Hebridean islands off the west coast of Scotland. There, girls from all over Scotland found lots of work in the summer herring season and, because of the many accidents with sharp knives that the girls used for gutting fish, there was also a lot of work for a good nurse like Mary Reddin.

The year was 1898 when James Liddell set sail from England and the whole of China was in turmoil. The young Emperor, Kuang Hsu, had opened up some old Buddhist temples to use as extra schools for Chinese children and his aunt was furious with him. She'd always believed him to be a traitor to his country. Now she feared the Dragon throne itself was in danger.

Kuang Hsu suspected his role as China's ruler was being threatened, perhaps even his life, so he arranged to have his aunt arrested and exiled to the Summer Palace where she could exercise no power.

Instead, the old Empress had *him* arrested as a traitor and banished to the very 'prison' he had planned for her. With him went the wife he hated, whom his aunt had chosen for him, while Pearl, the wife he loved, was thrown to her death down a well.

The Summer Palace stood on an island in the Lake of Pure Rippling Waves in the Forbidden City. It wasn't a *prison* at all except in the sense that the Emperor was never allowed to leave it. Close by the Summer Palace, moored in the lake, was a full-sized replica of a Mississippi paddle steamer constructed in pure white marble. Here the little old Empress used to spend long, sunny afternoons much to her nephew's annoyance. Kuang Hsu knew that she had paid for it with money that was given her to spend for the benefit of China's poor people.

With Kuang Hsu out of the way, T'zu Hsi, at the age of sixty-three, took control of the Chinese Empire for the third time in her life. More than ever she was determined to rid the land of aliens, and most of all, their Christianity – and the dreaded secret society of Boxers came out in open revolt to side with her.

The whole world sensed that a great rebellion was simmering in China and it was only a question of when would it erupt.

James knew all of this before he sailed but he didn't know as much about China and her people as he thought he did.

He'd always believed they were a small race of people and was surprised to see that northerners were quite tall. They were rather slow in their movements and neither as talkative or excitable as he'd expected. It was a shock to learn of the little value they put on life. Peopled tended to care for themselves only. Beggars could starve in the street. No one cared or even seemed to notice. Beggars were of no importance.

Animals were as nothing and a dog lying in the street was as likely to be kicked by a passer-by as would a stone or an old tin can. In fact there was more pleasure in kicking an animal. Stones and tin cans don't squeal.

Girls were treated much the same as animals, sometimes worse. A man cared more for his mule than his daughters. They were of no value at all. Girls were often killed at birth or just put out in the street to die. No one saw anything wrong in this. They were only girls, after all.

Often missionary families or Chinese Christian converts would take these abandoned children into their own homes. They would even buy a girl slave from her owner. Trading in human beings is something no Christian would ever gladly do. Yet, in these circumstances it was the only way to save a young girl from a terrible life – or death.

When missionaries first worked in China they were simply concerned with bringing the teachings of Christ into the country. But eventually they introduced education and modern medicine. For the first time hospitals and clinics were available to the peasants.

Schools were built for the poor and girls were encouraged to attend too. Until then, not even the richest Chinese bothered to educate their daughters.

James soon discovered the most difficult part of his studies was in learning the Chinese language. Without this he could not hope to pass his final exams.

There were almost two languages, one for the highly educated, another for those who had never learned to read or write but simply *spoke* the language.

The language has 50,000 characters but it is only the most scholarly who know them all and this is called *'kwan hwa'*. But even children need to know at least 3,000 characters before they can speak the most basic Chinese and this is called *'wen hwa'*. We need to know only 26 letters to discover our entire language.

James was so determined to succeed that to everyone's surprise, and especially his own, he learned *'wen hwa'* Chinese within his first year there. Still, in all, it had taken him six long years to complete his training – first as a church minister and finally as a missionary.

2: The Missionaries

Over a year had passed since James left Scotland to the time when the London Mission Society gave Mary permission to go to China.

Whenever news of China's troubles had reached her on the Hebridean island, her heart was filled with anxiety for James and joy was mixed with fear at the prospect of going there herself.

In his letters, James told her of what a miserable place Mongolia was with its high mountains and vast, arid deserts. There were very few towns and not many people. The Mongols were mostly nomads – wanderers who never settle anywhere. They were all herdsmen with goats, sheep, horses and camels. No crops were grown because no one stayed anywhere long enough to tend them.

The mission post was a proper building – made of clay – but the Mongols themselves all lived in *yurts*. These are houses shaped like an Eskimo igloo but constructed of poles and thick layers of felt. They are easily erected and dismantled so they can be packed on to a camel's back and transported to the next dwelling place.

James found the Mongols a strange people with their deep yellow skins, and eyes even more slanted than the Chinese. It is believed this comes from living amid the yellow sand and from screwing up their eyes against the desert sand and dust. Furthermore, Mongolia always seemed to be freezing.

Still, Mary had promised to 'follow him to the ends of the earth'. With a heavy heart at leaving the land of her birth and the people she loved, she set sail, leaving everything familiar to face a new life on the far side of the world. But there was happiness too. She was to be a Christian missionary's wife and she was sure her life partner had been especially chosen for her by the Lord himself.

James made the long journey south from Mongolia to meet Mary when she arrived in Shanghai, the great trading post of the east and China's biggest city. Shanghai lies fifty miles from the sea and can only be reached by sailing along the Huang Pu, a small tributary of the river Yangtse. There was early evidence of the land to which she had travelled when the ship passed dozens of sampans, bobbing about on the water. But Mary was astonished when she disembarked from her ship. Nearly all the buildings in Shanghai were European in style. Many of them Mock Tudor. Everywhere were statues to great men of the West. And in 'The Bund', the city's main street, familiar names stood out over hotels, banks and stores.

How happy she was to see James again after the long wait and the worry. He soon showed her a different Shanghai though. This was known as 'the old town' and it was here where the poorer Chinese lived. There were no plush hotels or splendid buildings.

In contrast to the smart stores on 'The Bund', there, shops consisted of a bamboo pole carried across the vendor's shoulders. Suspended from each end of the pole were two baskets in which he carried his wares.

Dressed in cotton trousers, loose fitting jacket and shallow, straw *coolie* hat, the man would trot along with his shop until he found a suitable place to stop and open up. Inside the baskets could be anything from foodstuffs to clothing. The man would sit waiting for customers, occasionally

19

swatting flies that dared to land on his goods. Even the barber traded this way, cutting hair and shaving his clients out in the street.

There was another odd aspect too. The customers gambled with the shopkeeper. After they'd decided what they wanted to buy or had had their hair barbered, the vendor would hold out a little bunch of thin twigs and the customer would give him a number. Then they drew out one of the twigs and if the number he'd given was the same as that on the stick, then the customer didn't pay.

James and Mary didn't approve of gambling but this really amused them.

James had made arrangements for a quiet wedding to be held in the beautiful Shanghai cathedral. It was for the 23rd of October, 1899; a time of autumn in their own native land and the happy day was tinged with sadness at the absence of all their loved ones. Still, they had their families' blessings and knew they were with them in spirit.

After the wedding the Reverend James Dunlop Liddell, with his bride, returned to his mission post in Mongolia. Mary was about to face a life she'd never imagined in all her wildest dreams because it was at this precise time that the notorious and long-awaited Boxer rebellion erupted.

The first attacks were on the northern mission posts in Mongolia, the very place where the Liddells were living.

The Fists of Righteous Harmony, to give the Boxers their proper name, believed they had magical powers and were sure they were possessed by the spirit of an ancient warrior which made them immortal.

They thought their bodies could stop bullets and cannonballs, even that they could make them turn and kill whoever had fired them. And they believed they could ward off a sword thrust with their bare arms. Of course, the simple, uneducated peasants accepted all this nonsense and went in terror of them.

The government claimed they were unable to stop the uprising but many government officials were actually helping it along.

Although many Chinese were bitterly opposed to having foreigners in their land, with a population of five hundred million, most of them peasants, there were also millions who *didn't* feel any of this hatred. Instead it was the wicked, little old Empress, T'zu Hsi whom they hated and feared most.

In the haven of the Forbidden City, with its dozen palaces, T'zu Hsi was pretending all the time to be a friend of the westerners. Dressed in beautifully embroidered satin robes she entertained ladies from the foreign embassies who she'd invited to tea. She would smile sweetly and even give them little gifts. If ever there was mention of the Boxers and their cruel acts against missionaries, she refused to discuss it. She said she doubted if such a society existed at all, yet all the time she was their greatest supporter.

With the Christian missionaries being so liked and respected by the peasants, thousands had been converted to Christianity. Now, in a time of rebellion, the converts' lives were in as much danger as any 'foreign devils'.

Within seven months, almost before James and Mary had settled either into their work or their marriage, along with several converts, they were running for their lives. Everything they owned had to be abandoned with the exception of one small case of clothing.

During their flight, danger loomed every day and around every corner. James constantly prayed for their safe arrival back in Shanghai as there was more to consider than their own safety. Mary was expecting a baby and the horrors of that journey accompanied by the threat of being killed – or worse, captured alive, were hardly what a pregnant woman should have been faced with.

Eventually, they did reach the coast and managed to get a ship back to Shanghai—the city where only a few months earlier, they had been married.

However, shortly after their arrival, that great city came under fire from the Boxers. It was a terrifying time. It was there, in the missionary compound on August 27th, 1900, while still under siege, that Mary gave birth to their first child, a son, Robert Victor.

Eventually, the rebels moved away to terrorise some other place. At last, after long days and sleepless nights of fear, the people of Shanghai were able to move about freely again and carry on with their normal lives.

When Robert was a few months old and able to travel, his parents started to make their way back towards their lonely mission post.

Since their flight to safety, there had been no word of the few people who had refused to leave the Mongolian mission. James was anxious to discover their fate at the hands of the murderous Boxers. They were still operating in large groups everywhere, committing barbarous atrocities against all foreigners or their Chinese friends.

Fearful of what he might find there and of what he may have to endure himself, James persuaded Mary to stay with baby Robert in Tientsin. From there, he made his hazardous journey back to Mongolia in the company of a Colonel Wei and some of his troops.

The rebels had destroyed all the railway, telephone and telegraph lines so there was no communication of any kind from James for the next four months and Mary was sick with worry. Was he dead or alive, she wondered? Nor were she and the baby in a safe place as James had believed.

Tientsin is a city only slightly smaller than Shanghai, but much further north—about eighty miles from the capital city, Peking, and not far from the Mongolian border.

22

After the Boxers' assault on the Mongolian mission outposts, they moved south to attack Peking. There was only a force of three hundred British troops to defend it. T'zu Hsi sat in the safety of the Forbidden City on the Dragon throne surrounded by ugly, carved stone beasts. They guarded the throne room itself and with all their superstitions, no Chinese would ever dare to enter. Because of this, the Empress could still deny any knowledge of the Fists of Righteous Harmony, yet Peking was burning. Buildings were rased to the ground. Their inhabitants either burned with them or ran out only to be beheaded.

After Peking, the next city on the Boxers list was Tientsin. It was a winter of great dread when no one knew what the next day, or even the next hour would bring.

Like most Chinese towns and cities, Tientsin was divided into two parts. One, the prosperous western side, the other made up of dark, narrow alleyways where people lived in miserable squalor. But at that time, they were all as one. Sandbags were quickly being filled and placed around all buildings in case they were shelled.

Always, rumours were coming in of the Boxers approach. In a village close by, two missionaries were brutally murdered. At Weihsien, a town near Peking, houses *and people* were set on fire. Weihsien was a place almost unknown to Mary but one day it would become the most important town in the world for her and the family.

It was on June 11th, that Sugiyama, the Japanese Chancellor went to stand in the Tientsin city gateway to look out over the land as yet more rumours had spread over the city. There was no sign of anyone lurking about until suddenly, a shot rang out and the Japanese Chancellor fell dead. The great gates were immediately swung to and from that moment on, Tientsin was under siege. The city walls became a trap for, although they prevented the Boxers from getting in, with the gates and walls constantly under fire, they also stopped anyone from leaving.

Many women and children had been evacuated from the city but some were unable to leave before the enemy arrived. Mary and her baby were among them. They were moved into a building along with other women and children from the foreign concession, but even that came under fire.

The city had a better defence than Peking though and this saved everyone from being massacred. Two thousand Russian troops had been making their way to the capital when they put in at Tientsin to rest and they were there when the Boxers arrived. They fought furiously for days until a British naval brigade sailed up the river and put up a frightening barrage. The Boxers knew they had lost the battle and decided to leave. At night, they set off fireworks all round the city walls to distract the defending troops who believed they were surrounded. As the Russian and British defenders shot in all directions, believing the fireworks to be gunfire, the Boxers escaped.

A third of Tientsin city was in flames by that time and James had thought he'd left his family in safety.

For a while after that, the women and children were taken aboard the British ships for protection in case the revolutionaries returned. But they didn't return. Instead they moved on to inflict more damage and unspeakable cruelties in other places.

When James had reached Mongolia he had found his mission post completely abandoned. There was nothing for him to do but start back for Tientsin. But the weather conditions and the threat of Boxers made it impossible, so he stayed with Colonel Wei in the hills and returned when they did.

When he reached Tientsin, he was horrified to hear all

that had happened and thanked the Lord for protecting his family in his absence.

By this time, the Boxer rebellion had been squashed by a combined force of 30,000 troops from all the western powers working together.

The Empress T'zu Hsi fled from Peking in a mule cart. Dressed as a peasant instead of in her Imperial robes and jewels, not even her own guards had recognised her as she passed through the great gateway of Peking.

The western powers insisted on the law being changed. From then on, anyone joining a secret society was to be executed immediately they were discovered. Heavy penalties were put on the Chinese government for damage to foreign buildings. They were made to pay a fine of 303 million pounds.

James no longer had a mission post to work in so they stayed in Tientsin until the London Mission Society sent him word of a new posting.

During their time there, they wached the city being rebuilt and modernised. More railway lines were opened up to improve communication between Tientsin and Peking and their surrounding districts. And there was to be a college in the city where English teachers would teach Chinese students.

James and Mary were still there in January, 1902 and baby Robert was one and a half years old when, on the 16th January, a brother was born. They were proud to have two sons. James hastened off to register the birth and stopped in the street to tell a missionary friend the good news.

'Well, Liddell, and what are you going to call the wee chap?' asked the friend.

'Henry Eric,' answered the happy father and went on his way until his friend called him back.

'*Henry Eric Liddell!* He'll have a hard time at school with those initials. Do you realise they spell HEL?' Hardly appropriate for a missionary's son, do you think?'

James was stunned. He hadn't given a thought to the initials. He raced back to Mary and told her. How she laughed. 'Well, just change the names round and call him Eric Henry instead,' she said. And so, their second son became Eric Henry Liddell.

Shortly after Eric's birth, James received his new posting. It was Siao Chang; very far away from his old post in Mongolia and as different as could possibly be.

It was one of thousands of tiny villages that stood on the Great Plain of China. To reach it meant facing a long and arduous journey; six hours by train followed by an overnight stop at an Inn. After this came a forty-mile trek in a mule-cart. Chinese trains were neither clean nor comfortable. And although forty miles seems a short distance, the roads were so bad that it took a full day in the ricketty, bumpy mule-cart which resulted in bruised flesh and aching bones.

Because of this, when James left, both he and Mary thought it wiser for her to stay on in Tientsin with the two babies until Eric was a little older. Once again James and Mary were separated. From being married they had constantly been on the move and in danger. At times, Mary asked the Lord if she would ever be able to settle down and make a real home for her husband and children. Of course, other missionaries were in the same situation and when they felt depressed they all tried to cheer each other up.

Finally, the time came to make the journey to Siao Chang. It was spring and the freezing, Tientsin winter was at an end. Some other missionaries were travelling with Mary and fortunately for her, they knew all about Chinese Inns. They explained that there would be no beds. Everyone

26

slept together on a k'ang – a square brick structure raised from the floor and kept warm by the ovens underneath where the food was cooked by day.

The k'angs were always swept clean but the warm ovens attracted all sorts of living insects. Mary didn't want her babies or herself to suffer from flea bites or any other verminous intruders that came in the night to creep into clothes and burrow under the skin of sleeping travellers. Much to the amusement of the Chinese, she and her companions took canvas camp-beds with them. They also took their own food and cooked it themselves in the Inns' brick ovens.

As the last forty miles were along hard, sun-baked tracks they set off early the following morning and reached Siao Chang late in the afternoon. Though her body was sore and she was weary, Mary felt that at long last her prayers had been answered. She and her little boys were reunited with James and they could finally settle down to be a complete family.

The first thing she noticed was a sign hanging over the village gate saying 'Chung Wai, I Chai'. James explained this meant, 'Chinese and Foreigners, All One Home'. It had been put there immediately after the villagers heard the Boxer rebellion was at an end. After the past years of danger, worry and horror, it was a most welcoming sight for Mary Liddell, the pretty, little girl who had promised to go to the ends of the earth.

3: Eric

Mary soon discovered that life on the Great China Plain was much easier than in Mongolia.

Mission work had been going on there for years. And, as the Bible had been translated into *wen hwa*, the peasants language, there were many Chinese Evangelist teachers at work on the Plain.

James' work was more that of a parish priest than a missionary and he was actually called Li Mu Shi – Pastor Liddell. Still, it was a very big parish to cover. For ten thousand villages holding ten million people, there were only two mission posts and Siao Chang was one of them.

Unlike more southerly places where the heavy rainfall was perfect for growing rice in the wet paddy-fields, Siao Chang was in a drought area. The land was always dry and dusty and the farmers were constantly irrigating their crops with river water to keep them alive. Temperatures were extreme. Summers were terribly hot and winters were freezing.

The Plain was a patchwork of fields, muddy rivers and tiny villages whose inhabitants were all farmers – or *han* to use their Chinese name.

Few trees grew except for the odd Tamarisk here and there. Animals were almost as rare as trees because they took up valuable grazing land when every piece was needed for crops, the people's main food.

All the same, there was one section of each farmer's field

that was never used for crops. This was his family burial ground and was always situated in the very centre of the best field to show how much his dead relatives were revered. It was an awful waste and made ploughing difficult but it was tradition and nothing could make them change.

The rest of the land was for growing peanuts, soya beans, sweet potatoes, millet, wheat and kaoliang, a form of wheat with stalks so thick they were used for making fences.

It was the worst famine area in the whole of China. The weather plays an important part in every farmer's life and they lived with almost constant drought. A hot, rainless June saw crops of winter wheat scorched or actually burnt up. And although they always needed rain badly, when it came it fell so heavily it did as much damage as the sun because it often washed the crops away.

Millet and wheat were the main summer cereals. But alongside them grew soya beans, sweet potatoes and peanuts. They all like dry weather and sandy soil. On the Plain they had both. No one could ever risk having a failed harvest so in really poor places, more sweet potatoes were grown than anything else. They were easier to grow and needed less attention. They were sown in May and harvested in October.

August and September were spent ploughing and seeding other crops. The Chinese year has thirteen months and this harvest began on the fifth day of the fifth month during the Festival of Tuan Wu – meaning double fifth. This is about our mid-June.

Nothing was wasted. From soya came tu fu, a bean curd. Tu-chiang was a milk made from the bean which was excellent for babies and invalids. Soya bean oil was used for cooking and light and whatever was left from the plant, after all that processing, was formed into large round cakes and sold for animal food.

29

Even the millet and wheat roots were dried and stored away to be used as heating fuel during the winter.

Unfortunately, snowfalls are usually light in that area. But if they got a heavy fall it acted as a blanket for the young shoots so if snow fell at New Year there was much rejoicing because it was the omen for a good summer harvest.

To keep up all the necessary food supplies, farmers, together with women and children, worked in the fields from dawn till dusk, seven days a week. They worked so hard they rarely left their village or its surrounding fields but they had a happy life.

Summer evenings would see people gathered in groups outside their mud-walled homes, indulging in two of China's favourite pastimes—telling stories and singing. Singing played a big part in their lives. They sang while they ploughed, seeded or harvested and the air was filled with music from morning till night.

Nothing delighted James and Mary more than to hear the hymns the peasants had learned being carried on the air to neighbouring fields where other workers would join in.

Inside the mission compound stood four big houses in a row with verandahs both upstairs and down and also at the back and front of each house. Behind these four houses were the church, the hospital and two schools; one for boys, one for girls. It was only the Christian missionaries who believed in girls' education.

Siao Chang's village wall was made of mud. It wasn't very strong nor was it high but it was so thick that people could walk along its top.

The village houses were all clustered together and, like the wall, they were built of mud. This mud wasn't made into bricks, but simply pressed together into clods and left to bake in the sun.

The roofs were made of straw and, on the rare occasion

when they had rain, they would let in water and the mud walls would get soft. Then the houses and the village wall could all collapse and slide down in a wet mess, leaving the village without protection and the people homeless.

The mud is called *loess* and is made up of a grey-yellow sand so fine that it can be rubbed into the skin like talcum powder. It is believed that loess is really the sand that is blown there from the Gobi Desert in Mongolia. When it lands on the Plain, it can build up to be anything from one metre to half a mile thick.

Loess stains everything it touches so wherever you look, all is a greyish yellow colour. During the frequent dust storms, it blows about and sticks to every surface, even vertical ones. In places it forms hills with steep, cliff-like faces. And, as the area is prone to earthquakes, if one occurs, a hill can disintegrate and bury a whole village. Even the rivers can bring devastation because the loess silts them up until they overflow, bringing killer floods.

Still, all these threats from nature were as nothing compared to the dangers the Liddells had experienced up to that time in China.

James and Mary had gone there prepared to face all sorts of people and hazards that came their way. Now they were thankful to know the worst times were over because they had been faced right at the beginning. In Siao Chang, the Lord had given them a life of contentment among people who genuinely liked them and wanted them there.

In the evening, as the village gatekeeper swung the mighty wooden gates shut and barred them, everyone in Siao Chang went to their beds in peace and happiness.

In October, 1903, just over a year after moving to the Plain, as the autumn was growing close to the icy winter, James and Mary's third child, Jenny, was born.

By that time, Robert was three years old and Eric was

31

aged twenty-one months. They were lively little boys and needed the company of other children. They were the only children living in the mission compound but they weren't without playmates. There were lots of small children in the village, too small to work in the fields, so they became the friends of Robert and Eric.

Wrapped up snugly against the cold in their thick, quilted Chinese coats and hoods, it was difficult to tell which were the Liddells and which children were Chinese as they raced about. They were taught all the games Chinese children played, ones they would never even have heard of if they lived in their parents' native country. As they grew older, they learned to play ping-pong and chess too.

Robert, or Robbie as he was called, and Eric grew up as familiar with the Chinese language as with English. It was their mother who had language problems but she was always learning, and sometimes from her own children.

Mary helped James a lot with his work so to help with caring for the children, the Liddells engaged an *amah* – a nanny, whose name was Gee Nai Nai. She wasn't very young but she gave them all her attention and loved them a lot. The children loved Gee Nai Nai too and there was always much laughter in the house especially when she had trouble saying their names. She called Eric, *Yellie*; Robbie was *Lordie* and their little sister, Jenny was *Jiernie*.

The children didn't seem to notice the difficulty their nanny had in walking. Like all Chinese women at that time, Gee Nai Nai's feet were bound up tight to prevent them from growing. This was a custom for all girls and women and was very cruel. Eventually it became illegal but not until many years later.

Just like most children, the Liddells longed to own pets, but with the ever-present danger of rabies in foreign lands, their parents couldn't allow them to have a dog or a cat.

One day a kitten did get into the house. Robbie and Eric raced round the dining-room trying to catch it with three-year-old Eric squealing 'Hsieo mao pao la' meaning 'the little cat has run away'.

James and Mary were so upset to see how they loved animals, they decided to let them adopt a family of goats from a nearby field. Robbie owned the billy; Eric the nanny and Jenny had the kid. These pets made them very happy until one day when Robbie's billy goat began to butt them all quite viciously. From that day on, the childrn weren't too keen to own pets and the goats were left alone in the field where they belonged.

Eric was a rather delicate child with fair hair, blue eyes and pale skin. In his padded coats he looked quite plump but he was really quite skinny. His mother nursed him and the others through many childhood illnesses, usually without a doctor in attendance. Of course, Mary was a trained nurse. Still, it always seemed to be Eric who was sick and he was always worse than the other two.

He was once so ill he couldn't eat food for a long time and survived on meat juice. Mary never left his bedside day or night and when he was better, it took a long time for him to walk again. His limbs were so stiff they had to be massaged every few hours and a lady who was visiting them upset Mary when she said, 'That boy will never be able to run again.' Of course, she was wrong and he made a complete recovery.

Perhaps the first indication of the man Eric Liddell would one day become was when another visitor went for a walk together with her husband, Mary, Robbie and Eric to the sandhils, as the children called them, which were really just build-ups of loess.

On this cold winter's day, while they were still some distance from the village, a north wind suddenly began to blow. There was such a fierce sand and dust storm they could hardly stay on their feet. There was no warning of its approach before it struck and there was no shelter. With the grown-ups clutching the children's hands, they all struggled against the intense wind and blinding dust to reach the village. Everyone coughed and choked. Their eyes streamed with stinging tears and Eric's little legs smarted as the dust particles found their way through his trouser legs. His body ached from holding himself against the cold and he was weary. On and on the party struggled, half-carrying, half-dragging the small boys. Suddenly, Eric broke loose from his mother's grip. He realised he was holding them back because he was the smallest and the weakest. With a sad expression on his face he said, 'It's far long. I'll have to be leaved.'

At such an early age, he was willing to sacrifice his life for the sake of others. His selfless thought only filled the others with determination and soon they were back in the warm safety of their home. But each one felt a special respect for the little boy.

His kind, sensitive nature often showed up in other ways too. The children loved to have their mother sit at the piano and play for them to sing and there was one song which Eric especially loved. It was the Moody and Sankey hymn 'The Ninety and Nine'. But when they reached the part where the little lamb was lost, Eric always began to cry and his sobs were louder than the voices of the singers.

One day, Mary sat at the piano and asked, 'Well, what shall we sing?'

'The Ninety and Nine', said Eric.

'Oh, no,' answered his mother. 'When we sing that, you always cry.'

Eric promised he wouldn't cry if only she would play it for him. But sure enough, as soon as they came to where the lamb was lost, Eric began to weep.

Mary turn round and said, 'Eric, you're crying after promising that you wouldn't.'

I'm n . . . n . . . not cr . . . crying,' sobbed Eric, 'I'm l . . . laughing.'

In fact, Eric did laugh a lot. Well, they were more giggling fits than laughing. Sometimes he was so bad his mother sent him from the room until he stopped. But Mary had such a sweet nature that when she tried to be angry with her children, it only made Eric giggle all the more.

The Liddells didn't spend all their time at Siao Chang. In the summer, when the heat was almost unbearable, the schools for the village children would close because the farmers were busy with their harvest and needed their help more than ever. Then, most missionaries took a holiday at Pei-Tai-Ho, a seaside resort not very far from Tientsin. It was a lovely place with a long, sandy beach that was overlooked by green hills. The wives and children spent about three months there with the men joining them in August when the farmers were at their busiest.

How the children looked forward to those holiday weeks when they could play on the beach and paddle at the water's edge. Mary taught them to swim and people were always arranging beach picnics to which everyone was invited. There were donkey rides, organised sports days and in the evenings there would be concerts or sing-songs.

James always loved the time spent there when he was able to put aside his work for a while and be with Mary and the children. With so many villages on the Plain for him to minister to, there were times when he was away from home for weeks.

Eric, Robbie and Jenny weren't sure what their father's work was. They knew he was a missionary and that they all lived in a mission post but they didn't understand what that meant.

Mary often had to remind them that most of what they saw around them belonged to the mission. One day when she found Eric up to mischief – hammering nails into the front verandah floor, she stopped him with 'You mustn't do that, Eric. It belongs to the mission.'

Her small son looked up and in a wistful voice asked, 'Do we belong to the mission?'

As they got older they began to notice that the Chinese people looked and dressed differently from the people living in the mission compound – all except themselves. They dressed just like the village children but they sensed they were different because they didn't wear long queues – pigtails. The people living inside the compound spoke Chinese *and* English while those outside spoke only Chinese. And the mission ladies didn't have bound feet.

The Liddells could eat with chopsticks and usually ate the same food as the farmers. This was something which would one day help Eric to survive. Yet, even with all these things in mind, the children accepted it as a normal way of life. It was, after all, the only one they knew.

Eighteen months after the Boxer rebellion had ended, the old Empress, T'zu Hsi, had been allowed to return to Peking and the Forbidden City Palaces. She came, no longer as a fugitive in disguise but in great splendour. Wearing her blue and gold Imperial robes she passed through the streets in a gold-brocade, curtained litter carried by four pole-bearers.

The western powers had shown much diplomacy and accepted her explanation that her reason for flight was fear of the Boxers. They knew this was untrue and there was anger in many hearts as the people lined the street to watch her ceremonial arrival.

Still, she had no real power any longer and, for a while, the Chinese people lived their lives unhindered by political squabbles.

In the year when Robbie Liddell had his seventh birthday, Eric his fifth and Jenny her third, their father, the Reverend James Dunlop Liddell, had been in China for nine years and his wife, Mary, for eight. At last, they were due for their first leave.

How their families in Scotland eagerly awaited their return with the three children they'd never seen. The children were also excited yet sad at leaving their mission home on the China Plain. There were tears when they made their farewells to Gee Nai Nai and their friends. Robbie and Eric were especially upset because they knew it would be many years before they returned to China.

The family travelled to Shanghai where they boarded a German liner for the six-week voyage to Britain and, within minutes, they were terribly confused at all the different languages on board. They were surrounded by Chinese, English, German and Scottish voices as well as many others. Some time later when they were back in Britain, when Mary was wondering where Eric was, he called in a strong Scots accent, 'I'm cooming doon the stairs.' Then he proudly announced that he had spoken German!

The liner docked at Southampton and the Liddells spent some days in London where their father was to report to the London Mission Society. London, with all its bustle and noise, was a bit frightening at first. But it wasn't long before they were on the train, heading north for Scotland and the little village of Drymen at the foot of Ben Lomond.

The villagers treated the returning grocer's son and his family like celebrities and James' family were overjoyed to have him home again with his wife and children. What they forgot was that only James and Mary had come home.

Robbie, Eric and Jenny were open-mouthed at the splendour of the mountains, heather and fir trees. They thought Loch Lomond was beautiful too, but for them

Scotland was a foreign country. Everything they saw was completely different from the dry, yellow Plain and the sandy beach at Pei-Tai-Ho.

As their leave was going to last a year, James and Mary rented a furnished house in the village and they got places for Robbie and Eric in the village school. The children soon grew used to their new family of aunts, uncles and cousins and when their grandparents began to tell them tales of their father's childhood they laughed and laughed. Before long they felt as much at home as their mother and father.

It was at the village school where they felt most strange. The other children thought the Liddells were Chinese and it took a while for them to realise they were as Scottish as they were. After a few weeks, Robbie and Eric had learned many new games and they had taught the Drymen children all the Chinese games they knew as well as many customs.

Eric soon discovered that 'Cooming doon the stairs' wasn't German at all. Unfortunately, he learned something else too – some awful swear words.

'Oh, Eric, you mustn't ever say that. It's a swear word,' his mother told him one day when he had come out with yet another word he shouldn't have even known.

Eric looked at her for a while in deep thought then he said, 'I know. You tell me all the swear words there are and then I'll know what I mustn't say.'

Mary tried to explain that she wasn't going to do anything of the sort and poor Eric had to learn by his own mistakes.

At the end of the year, when it was time for James to return to China, the children had grown to love all their Scottish relatives and felt quite at home there, which was a good thing because *they* weren't going back to China.

It was usual for missionaries' children to be educated in

their own native country. This was for several reasons. Their fathers were often moved about from post to post and this had a very unsettling effect on their children. Another reason was that there weren't always schools available except those run by missionaries where they would only receive a basic education.

The London Mission Society had its own school for their missionaries' children and this was where Robbie and Eric were to go.

The children hated their father leaving them. Still their mother was staying with them for another year to get them settled into boarding school. Mary realised it was going to be an ordeal for Robbie, aged eight, and Eric, aged six. They would be left in a strange land with no family close to them.

When the time came for them to leave Scotland for their new school in London, they all said tearful 'Goodbyes' to everyone in Drymen village. Then the two boys with their mother and Jenny set off on the train for a new life.

It was a strange journey. Whenever they thought of the little village nestling close to Loch Lomond they felt sad. Then they would be upset at the thought of Mary and Jenny going back to China without them. In the next instant, all three children would see something interesting through the carriage window as it sped south. Filled with curiosity, they would press their faces up against the glass and all sadness would be forgotten for a while.

All through that journey, Mary was heartbroken but she didn't show it. She was thankful the boys didn't realise just how long it would be before they saw their parents again. At eight and six, they couldn't imagine time in terms of years.

And Mary herself was going back to a different China from the one she'd left a year earlier. The London Mission Society had given James a new posting in Peking, the capital city. And there had been great changes there. While in Scotland, they'd heard of the death of the Emperor Kuang Hsu and of his hated aunt, the dowager Empress T'zu Hsi.

The new Emperor of China was P'u-yi, a two-year-old boy. But this time there would be no Regency. China was no longer recognised as an Imperial power and the Emperor was merely a 'puppet ruler' – a ruler in name only.

Again the whole country was in a state of upheaval and on the brink of yet another revolution.

Wistfully, Mary recalled the happy years in Siao Chang with her family and wished for them back. She instantly dismissed the idea from her mind. She had chosen to be a missionary's wife and must accept whatever came.

4: Schooldays

The school was at Blackheath in the south-east corner of London. It was called The School for the Sons of Missionaries and David Livingstone's son had once been a pupil there.

Just as in most boys' schools at that time there was a lot of bullying and 'ragging', a schoolboys' word for tormenting.

All new boys had to face an initiation – a form of welcome from the other pupils which did anything but make the newcomer feel welcome.

In that particular school it took the form of 'running the gauntlet'. Two teams lined up facing each other, each boy armed with a knotted handkerchief. As the new arrival ran between them he was lashed by these weapons. It wasn't a very harsh initiation ceremony. Other schools had much worse and although these rituals were against the rules and supposed to be done in secret, the teachers knew all about them.

It was only when the knot in the handkerchief hit a tender spot on the body that it hurt and, of course, any boy with a cruel streak always aimed for the head, face, hands or legs. In those days, boys wore short trousers until they were nearing manhood so there was a lot of bare flesh to aim for.

Robbie and Eric took their 'ragging' well and showed the same spirit as when they said 'Goodbye' to their mother and Jenny a few months later.

Eric was so unlike his fellow pupils with his frail body

and poor health that his mother worried more about leaving him than Robbie.

His headmaster was rather concerned about this thin, pale, shy pupil too but he was a great believer in fresh air and sport which he felt was next to Godliness. 'Healthy minds in healthy bodies' was his unwritten rule and he was soon proved right.

Eric thrived during his first term there and when the end-of-term holiday came around he soon showed Mary she had nothing to worry about. She had taken a small house in London for the last remaining months of her stay in Britain. When the boys joined her there for their holiday she was delighted to see how Eric had improved in his physique. He'd gained in self-confidence too.

As well as initiation ceremonies, there was another tradition in boys' schools – fagging. This was when older boys took advantage of the 'freshmen' as they called them.

Under threat of a beating, they made them run errands, clean their shoes for them, tidy their rooms and even write out hundreds of detention lines they were supposed to do themselves as a punishment.

On Eric's first night home he sat in his chair, thrust out his feet and looking at his little sister asked 'Who'll be my fag?'

Jenny ran forward, eager to do her brother's bidding and clean his shoes. But Mary wisely stopped her from being her brother's servant and made him clean them himself.

When the time came for the final parting, the brothers were very brave. It was their mother who fought back the tears as she said 'Goodbye' to them in the headmaster's study just before they went out to play cricket.

Sadly, she followed them and, for a while, unable to tear herself away, she watched her small sons. After a few minutes and after she'd said a silent prayer for their safety and happiness she walked away.

Robbie and Eric were already involved in their cricket and didn't even notice that she'd gone. But that night, Eric cried himself to sleep.

Eric's health continued to improve as the weeks went on and he was soon as robust as any other boy in school. Autumn and winter terms say him playing rugby four times each week. In spring and summer he was playing cricket by day and in the evenings too just for recreation.

He was still shy and quiet compared to the rest and everyone called him 'the mouse'. Oddly enough, when the school play was put on in his second year and it happened to be *Alice in Wonderland*, Eric was chosen to play the dormouse. He gave a brilliant performance and in show business terms he brought the house down. This helped him to overcome a lot of his shyness and he wasn't as quiet after that.

The school may have been for the Sons of Missionaries but this didn't mean they were angelic. And, as Eric's shyness ebbed away, he got involved in all sorts of mischief, both inside the school and in the playground. Yet, he was always ready to own up if caught and never got anyone else into trouble even though they were involved in whatever prank he'd been caught at.

There was one night when the boys were behaving like anything other than Christian missionaries' sons and decided on a very dangerous game.

A big linen basket was smuggled into the dormitory and suspended outside the window on one of the building's upper floors. It was secured by a rope tied to a bed leg then a volunteer climbed into the basket. While his friends slowly let it down to the ground, one of them read the Order for the Burial of the Dead at Sea.

No one ever discovered which part Eric played in that particularly dangerous escapade but he made no secret that he was there all right. They were found out and all severely punished because the boy in the basket had been lucky to escape with his life.

Everyone hated school meals. Breakfast was bread and butter with porridge. Supper was worse – a huge hunk of bread and dripping. But the dish they dreaded most was when they were given dripping on suet pudding for lunch. Eric would rather have eaten a bowl of millet or soya beans, something he'd been used to in Siao Chiang. One day, he simply couldn't eat it. But he wasn't permitted to leave it either so he held the food in his mouth until he left the dining-hall. Once in the classroom, he spat it into the waste-paper basket and got caught doing it. Again he was punished.

He was often getting into trouble but his twinkling eyes and cheeky smile got him out of a lot too. However, despite his tricks and mischief, he was always kind to others.

When a new boy of seven had to go through the 'ragging', Eric lined up with the rest with his knotted handkerchief at the ready. Suddenly, the little boy became so terrified, wondering what was going to happen to him, he began to cry. Eric himself was only eight but he felt so sorry for the boy, he stepped forward, raised his hand and ordered that the 'ragging' be stopped. Somehow everyone sensed his authority and even the older boys stopped their shouting and jeering, lowered their handkerchiefs and walked away.

Although everyone liked Eric he was always a bit of a loner and never had a close friend except for his brother, Robbie. They were inseparable.

Eric was only of average ability in his studies but he shone on the playing fields – and so did Robbie.

Whenever they wrote to their parents in China, James and Mary always laughed to read how close and how fond of each other the brothers were, yet they were each other's greatest rival in sport.

James had always been good at sport, especially gymnastics and it seemed clear he'd passed his ability on to his sons. At this point in their young lives, it wasn't clear that he had passed on his love of Christ too.

Robbie and Eric were to travel north to spend the long, summer holidays with their relatives in Scotland. But because of the distance and expensive rail fare, they would have to spend their other holidays at the school.

This made it a very long school year yet, in a sense, they were better off spending Christmas there than in Drymen village. At that time, Scotland celebrated Christ's birth in great solemnity. They didn't rejoice with parties, greetings-cards, trees and gifts. All the fun was saved for the following week when they saw in the New Year or Hogmany as they call it.

As most pupils were in the same situation because their parents were working abroad, it brought all the boys in school closer together. At weekends and holiday periods it was more like a family home than a school.

There were pupils who had relatives living close to London and there were always some who had their parents home on leave. This meant they would invite school friends to stay with them for the holidays and the Liddell boys were often asked to stay in different homes with different families.

In 1911, when they had been at school for two years and Eric was aged nine, there was another revolution in China led by Sun-Yat-Sen. His aim was to turn China into a republic and he was successful. The following year, he was made president and the six-year-old Emperor, P'u-yi, was exiled in the Forbidden City Palaces. Once the country was formally proclaimed to be a republic, down came the familiar old yellow flag displaying the dragon rampant. In its place was a five-barred yellow, red, white, blue and black standard showing that Sun-Yat-Sen was the new leader.

In that same year, 1912, when Eric was ten, there was to be a big change in his life too. The school moved to more modern buildings in another part of London. It had been the Royal Naval School and was much bigger than the old one with spacious rooms and vast playing fields.

After moving, the next big change was in its name. It wouldn't be known as the School for the Sons of Missionaries. Its new title would simply be Eltham College. The reason for this was, with so much extra space, there was room for more pupils, so day boys were taken in and they didn't have to be sons of missionaries.

Eltham had its own library, hospital, workshops and science laboratory. It also had its own chapel which was a great improvement. Until then, boys had to walk miles in different directions to attend churches of various denominations.

Having day pupils from homes in the college district meant the boys had more contact with the outside world. They were no longer an isolated community and were encouraged to take part in activities that would never have been allowed before.

They went on excursions to the Royal Mint at Tower Hill to see how the nation's money was manufactured. They visited the Royal Observatory at Greenwich; went to see the county cricket matches at Lords and went for regular swimming sessions at the public baths.

Robbie and Eric loved doing all these things. All, that is, except one. Walthamstow Hall was a girls' school and sister college to Eltham but when the Eltham boys were invited over for a day to play tennis, much as Eric loved the game, he was too shy to go.

Like missionaries' children the world over, wealth was unknown to them and they were used to scraping pennies together for anything they wanted. When one of the new day boys asked the entire school to his home for a day, it was a rare treat. But when they arrived, it turned out to be an even greater treat than they'd expected. The boy's father was a market gardener who owned strawberry fields and as strawberries were at the end of their season, he wanted the boys to help clear his fields by picking and eating as many as they wanted. This became an annual event and one they looked forward to most of all.

There were 126 missionaries' sons, 14 boarders whose parents weren't missionaries and 46 day boys whose parents lived locally; traders, farmers and such. Robbie and Eric were settled into school, doing well at their studies and particularly at sport. They received letters from their parents quite often and were pleased when one arrived to tell them they had a new baby brother, Ernest. Mary was due to come home for a visit the following year, 1915 and the boys could barely wait to see her, Jenny and the baby.

But before the year 1914 was out, just as Robbie was 14 and Eric nearing his thirteenth birthday, the world erupted in the first World War. Every day dreadful news was reaching England of what was happening in France and Belgium.

James and Mary were desperately worried for their young sons at home in England. When the time came for Mary to leave China, she didn't know what to expect when she arrived home.

Robbie and Eric were overjoyed when she arrived with the baby. It seemed strange having a brother they'd never seen. Still, even Jenny was like a stranger – she'd grown so much since their last meeting seven years earlier.

Again Mary rented a house in London and the boys loved having a home of their own to go to every evening. For the time being they had become day boys while their mother was in London.

It was a short holiday, because in the early spring of 1916, weeks after Eric turned fourteen, she had to return to China.

James and Mary prayed as the war dragged on through 1916, 1917 and 1918, each year taking their sons closer to the age when they would be in uniform and facing the horrors of war. They'd experienced war themselves in China and hoped the Lord would spare the boys from such an ordeal.

Some of the older pupils were leaving school to go straight into uniform. And within a matter of weeks, word would come that they had been killed or maimed on the battlefields. Each morning at assembly, names were read out and prayers said either for their speedy recovery or in some cases, that their souls should rest in peace. It was horrible for the young pupils when they remembered these were the names of boys they'd been cheering on the playing fields only weeks before.

With so many leaving Eltham to do their duty in foreign lands, it meant the young boys were needed to do their duty – on the playing fields. Eric was put in the rugby team when he was only 14 and, in the same year, he won a prize for cricket, a game he didn't really like. But already his sports prowess was beginning to show.

Fortunately, the war ended in 1918 when Robbie wasn't quite 18 and Eric was sixteen. Robbie was only weeks away from enlistment age.

By then, Eric was vice-captain of the cricket team. A year later he was captain. All this time he was excelling at 'rugger' and was captaining that team as well in the same year. In between those activities, he managed to keep up with his studies and be a prefect.

Athletics was his favourite when it came to sport but he didn't have things all his own way. In the year he was prefect as well as captain of the cricket and rugby teams the schools athletics record read thus:

Cross Country	1st R Liddell	2nd E H Liddell
Long Jump	1st E H Liddell	2nd R Liddell
High Jump	1st R Liddell	2nd E H Liddell
100 yards	1st E H Liddell	2nd R Liddell
Hurdle Race	1st R Liddell	2nd E H Liddell
Quarter Mile	1st E H Liddell	2nd R Liddell

Eric's time of 10.2 seconds for the 100 yards set up a new record which is still unbroken.

That year saw him as Senior Athletic Champion and he was presented with the Blackheath Cup — an award that had followed on from the old school.

He held the same position again the next year but he didn't receive the award a second time as it can only be presented once to any one pupil.

None of this went to Eric's head. He just accepted it all as something he'd worked for. Arrogance and pomposity were two faults he couldn't tolerate in anyone, and with his sense of humour he always managed to deflate an arrogant person — even overbearing teachers — by saying something cutting then following it with a sweet smile so that they were never sure if he'd insulted them or not.

On being ordered about by anyone who was 'full of their own importance' as he called it, he would look straight at them and say 'Yes, *sir*.'

Although he was now a young man and had a face like an angel, he still got into all sorts of scrapes. He really had the most impish smile and his eyes twinkled with merriment. On one occasion, his headmaster, George Robertson, who had never suspected Eric of being capable of mischief, just happened to catch a glint in his eye as he passed. He stopped, turned and looked closely at him saying, 'Liddell. I'm beginning to think you are not as good as you look.'

'Liddell' proved it a few days later.

Eltham had a strict rule against anyone riding bicycles in the quadrangle. But one afternoon, when no one was about, of all people, the headmaster came riding through the 'quad' on his bike – and with his small son in the basket on the front.

Eric just happened to be glancing through the window in his study as the head rode through the archway and into the quadrangle. As he passed below Eric's window, he simply couldn't resist the temptation to call out 'Hey! No cycling there.'

George Robertson nearly fell off his bike with shock. And though it was he who had broken the rule, it was 'Liddell' who was sent to his dormitory for the rest of the day as a punishment.

Regular Bible classes were held at the college but no one was forced to attend them. The classes were merely there for anyone who wanted to go and Eric never missed one.

As he began to shine even more at sport there was another light beginning to glow within him. It burned fiercely with love for God and all things good and wholesome. Yet, he never spoke to anyone of how he felt.

At the Bible class, he would quietly walk in and take his seat to settle down and listen. After the master had finished speaking, he always invited the class to open up a discussion giving their opinion on what he'd said.

Eric never once got involved in these talks. Occasionally he would nod or smile in agreement at something but no more. Some wondered why he went there in the first place. But later, in the privacy of his bed, he would lie with folded arms propping the back of his head and go over in his mind all that he'd heard and would form his own opinions.

Missionaries' children seldom follow their parents into their lifes' work. It's more usual for them to want to do something entirely different. In this matter, Eltham wasn't like other such schools. More boys left to do missionary work than from any other school in Britain. Even so, Robbie wanted to be a doctor but Eric knew from childhood that he wanted the same work as his father.

The two brothers never tired of hearing about missionary work abroad. The school library always had the latest edition of all the missionary magazines and the Liddells always read from cover to cover, the one from the Anglo-Chinese Christian College in Tientsin. Not only did it keep them in touch with China, which was after all the land of their birth; it seemed to bring their parents a little closer.

The Principal of the Anglo-Chinese College in Tientsin was a close friend of Eltham's headmaster and whenever he was home on leave he always visited Eltham to preach in the school chapel. For Robbie and Eric this was even better than reading the magazines.

The year after the war ended, Robbie left Eltham to take up medical studies at Edinburgh University. The parting from Eric was very painful. Being away from James and Mary for so many years had made the boys feel closer than most brothers.

Still it would only be a year before Eric was joining him to take up his science studies. But when the time came he still needed one subject – French – to qualify for entrance to the University.

The year was 1920, just one year before James was due for leave and Mary was coming home early to set up a home for them.

As the train drew in at Waverly Station in Edinburgh, Mary could scarcely believe that the two, handsome young men standing on the platform were her own sons. In the five years since she'd last seen them, they'd left all signs of childhood behind.

It was such a joyous homecoming for them all. Jenny was

quite a young lady as, from the scrawny twelve year-old they'd said 'Goodbye' to, she'd grown into an attractive seventeen year-old. Ernest, the baby of the family, was now a schoolboy. It was a little sad that he didn't remember his big brothers at all but that was soon overcome.

Mary found a large house in a quiet Edinburgh street and once again, they were all living together under the same roof. The following year, James came home for the first time in twelve years. The change in his sons was even greater for him. They parted when Robbie was eight and Eric six. Now they were twenty-one and nineteen years old.

Because it was so long since his last home leave, he was going to be in Scotland for a very long holiday. This gave the boys and their father lots of time to get to know each other all over again.

It also gave Eric the chance to study for his necessary qualification. Now that he had a home, he engaged a private tutor to coach him in his French. But of course, this took money and that was always in short supply. To solve that problem, he took a summer job working on a farm just outside the city. It meant him being up at 6.0 a.m., grabbing a bit of breakfast then cycling off to work. By evening he was tired out but this is when he did all his studying.

It was a hard time for him, especially when it should really have been his summer holidays before University. However, by the end of the summer, it had all proved worthwhile. He was admitted to the University and went off with his brother to complete his education.

Now was the time when Eric's life appeared to be taking a different path from the one it had seemed the Lord was leading him along.

5: The Sportsman

After matriculating for a BSc, Eric had been at the University five months when a friend asked him about taking part in a sporting event. The University Athletic Sports Meeting was due to take place on the last Saturday in May, and as he'd heard of Eric's prowess on the track, he was sure he would be interested in the 100 yards race.

To his surprise, Eric wasn't. The Athletic meeting was only six weeks away and he was much too busy studying to take time off for training. However, the friend was very persuasive. He convinced Eric that he needed some relaxation or other interest away from his academic studies and Eric agreed.

He'd been good on the running track at Eltham but that was very different from the Edinburgh University Athletic Club. There he would be running in public and a professional ability was expected. The friend who had persuaded him to take part offered to train him although he didn't know much about it himself. However, the two liked each other a lot and they decided they'd do their best.

But during one of the training sessions, Eric told him that in the Easter holiday, just five weeks before the meeting, he was going on a six-day cycling tour with four other friends.

His trainer was horrified and argued that if he went he wouldn't be able to run when he got back. All the cycling would cause his muscles to seize up. As they were both only novices Eric thought he knew as much as his trainer and argued back that he would be all right.

When the time came, the five cyclists set off early on the Monday morning. Their destination was Ben Nevis, the highest mountain in Scotland. They'd been told of the incredible beauty they would see stretching out in front of them when they reached the summit. They had intended to stand there at dawn and watch the sun rise. After days of cycling it was a bitter disappointment to be at that very spot on a day overcast with black cloud and the sun blotted from their sight. Still, when they arrived back in Edinburgh the following Saturday morning, they all agreed it had been an enjoyable trip.

But Eric was in for another disappointment. His trainer had been right. When he went out to resume his training programme the next morning, all the spring had gone out of his muscles and his limbs were very stiff.

There were only four weeks to the last Saturday in May, the day he was to run in the University Athletics – and in public too he reminded himself. This wasn't merely a school sports day. He simply had to be fit and ready or he would 'let the side down'. No true sportsman would do that, just as he wouldn't have let his friends down after promising to go to Ben Nevis with them.

He exercised and trained, and he allowed his body to be massaged to a point where it became agonising. By the end of the four weeks, both Eric and his trainer were reasonably satisfied with his progress.

The great day came – a day when Eric Liddell wasn't competing with R Liddell but with a very different rival. Innes Stewart was running against him in the first heat, and he was expected to become Scottish champion.

In his white vest and unfashionable, much too long, black shorts, Eric lined up with the other competitors. It was a hot summer's day and the grass track had an uphill incline. The crowd were sure their idol, Innes, had no competition in the 100 yards race. And as the starting pistol sounded the off, their belief was strengthened when Innes Stewart took the lead. Then to everyone's surprise, he was caught up. Eric Liddell kept pace with him all the way to the tape when Stewart just managed to beat him by a couple of inches.

The first three in each heat qualified for the final later that afternoon. At the time of the final, the sun was beating down but the heat didn't stop Eric Liddell. He beat Scotland's great hope for the future by two inches.

Innes Stewart wasn't too dismayed. The 220 yards (furlong) was his best distance and he knew no one could beat him in that. Again the competitors lined up and this time it was Eric who sprang into the lead, gaining two yards right from the off. He held that position to the very end when Stewart put on a sudden spurt and made the tape by *one inch*.

The crowd went wild with glee and there were no ill feelings from Stewart for his challenger. He respected this University freshman with his little experience and applauded as loudly as anyone when Liddell received second prize for that day's racing.

But now, for Eric, it was back to his studies, or so he thought until it was pointed out that his performance that day gave him a place in the Scottish Inter Varsity Sports.

He knew it was an obligation he must honour and he was naturally delighted at his achievement on that hot day in May, 1921. He would have been stunned if anyone could have told him then that this was the only time he would take second prize.

From then on, he won *every* single race he ever ran in Scotland.

Although he returned to his studies, he also had to embark on even more rigorous training sessions. At Powderhall, the Edinburgh greyhound racing stadium, there was a cinder track. Eric had never seen a greyhound stadium nor a cinder track but his trainer explained that this was where all the professional athletes trained.

The first time he went, he couldn't believe his eyes and he couldn't keep a straight face. Everyone took it as such a serious business but with Eric's sense of humour it was more like a comedy show.

On one side of the arena, dogs were barking and yelping as they trained, while on the other side, Eric was practising his sprinting and starts.

It was also the first time he'd seen professional athletes training. There were no such things as tracksuits then and, as the evening was cold, the trainees wore their overcoats over their knee-length shorts. With their hairy legs and knobbly knees showing below the elegant tweeds and melton cloths, Eric thought they looked ridiculous. Whenever they began heaving and relaxing their shoulders then hopping and dancing about on their toes, Eric burst into a fit of giggles and kept bending down, pretending to adjust his socks. When they broke into short dashes over the track, he turned his back on them and covered his face with his hands so they wouldn't see him laughing.

That night, he told his family he would never make such a foolish spectacle of himself. But it wasn't long before he realised the value of such odd antics. Warming-up exercises before running a race was the way to prevent the agonising stiffness he'd suffered in the past, especially after his six-day cycle tour.

His amateur trainer friend knew, if Eric was to reach the necessary standard for the forthcoming Inter Varsity Sports Meeting, he would need *professional* coaching, which was something he wasn't capable of giving.

Fortunately, such a person was taking an interest in this promising newcomer.

Tom McKerchar was already putting other athletes through some rugged practice at Powderhall so he offered to take Eric in hand. He wouldn't act merely as his coach but also as his masseur.

But the first time Tom watched Eric closely while he was doing some running exercises, he was appalled at the way he stopped dead on reaching the tape.

'Never do that,' he yelled, 'you'll snap a muscle!'

From a distance, he'd had the impression that Eric was tall but he was only of average height at five feet nine inches. When he ran, his head rested on his shoulders with him gazing up at the heavens instead of where he was going. His knees came right up as though he was trying to hit his own chin and his feet were lifted far too high off the ground. His arms waved about all over the place and his fists punched out at the air making him look more like a boxer than a runner.

Tom McKerchar groaned inwardly, wondering if he'd made a big mistake in offering to coach such a hopeless case. Nevertheless, he had to admit that the boy kept winning races. There must be *some* hope for him even if he does resemble a dancing circus pony, he thought.

Under all this criticism, Eric's enthusiasm was slightly subdued. He placed himself in Tom's care, only to be taken back to the very beginning; learning all he'd missed the first time around.

He ceased to feel embarrassed when dancing about on his toes or performing any other comic ritual prior to running. For all his shyness he realised that training was a serious business and no one was looking, much less laughing at him.

He also learned that it was unwise to indulge in a heavy

57

meal before either a race or a training session. Even if he did almost choke himself trying to get the food down in the first place, excitement prevented it from digesting once he'd eaten it and it lay heavy on his stomach for hours.

Then there was the massage. His flesh and joints were pummelled tortuously. Yet, after each treatment he felt strangely relaxed and his muscles were getting more and more flexible. He found it boring constantly doing the same exercises so another lesson he needed to learn was patience.

But the hardest lesson of all was one he admitted years later that he never did master. This was his slowness in getting off at the start. There were no starting blocks in those days. The nearest thing to one was a deep hole bored in the ground by the runner's toes. Then, with the front part of the foot embedded in this crude 'block', the athlete waited for the pistol shot.

Time and time again, someone would make a false start and everyone would be brought back into line. Ths could go on for an entire training bout, ending in frayed nerves and tempers, but not from Eric. Exasperated though he was, he never complained. He was usually the culprit anyway.

As the days went by, Tom McKerchar grew to know his *protégé* well and sensed there was something more than a great athlete in Eric. Underneath all the smiles, the quiet jokes and the shyness, there was much more – a great man. Far from honouring Eric in giving him free coaching, Tom felt he was honoured to give it.

When the Inter Varsity Sports Day came along, all the gruelling effort proved worthwhile. Edinburgh beat Aberdeen, Glasgow and Fife Universities when, in two sprints, Eric Liddell and Innes Stewart got first and second places.

From then on, Eric won race after race in so many events

it would take a separate book to record them all. And on the subject of records, he broke one after another, some standing for many years.

During the first season of his sporting career his family was still on leave and he was living with them in their rented Edinburgh home. But this turned out to be a problem for his mother and Jenny.

There was never a week when he didn't arrive home with prizes. Of course, every successful sportsman or woman accumulates gold and silver cups, medals and rose-bowls – and the silver needs cleaning regularly. But as well as all those usual trophies, Eric was winning cases and cases of cutlery. There were cake stands, trays, platters, salad-bowls and servers: cake servers, fruit bowls, a silver tea set and kettle on a tray, brush and comb sets, cuff links, tiepins, vases, sets of leather luggage, big clocks, little clocks, silver or gold wristwatches and pocket watches on chains and more fountain pens and propelling pencils than the entire family would ever be able to use.

Naturally, Mary Liddell and her daughter were proud of him, even though they were the ones who had to clean it all but they were very concerned about it too. They looked forward to him arriving home after a race, yet in another way they dreaded it wondering what on earth he would bring home next. Where could they put it?

Looking for places to display or simply store the prizes was bad enough. But with so much silver and gold in the house and with Eric's name and address always appearing in the newspapers and sports magazines, they were afraid of burglars. For safety, every night they collected all the trophies from the shelves, tables and dressers and hid them under the beds, only to bring them out again the following morning.

Of course, Eric always came home with his eyes twinkling

and with that impish grin spread across his face which somehow made everything all right.

As well as his reputation as a runner, Eric was building up a name for himself in rugby circles.

November 1921 saw him on tour with the University team in south-east England, playing against Cambridge University and the United Hospitals in London. He was centre-three-quarter and in his first two trial games, he'd scored ten tries.

In seven matches, Eric's team won six of them and it wasn't long before he'd moved on from University and Inter Varsity Matches to International standard. When Scotland played Wales at Cardiff they won for the first time in 33 years (since 1890). After the match, the famous winger – for this is the position he'd moved into – was carried shoulder-high from the field by his team mates.

Many similar events followed and a year later, in 1922, ironically, he thought he'd scored his highest achievement when he played in France at the great Colombes Stadium in Paris. Who could know just what would happen in that same arena two years later?

Actually, Eric preferred rugby to running, yet it was his skill on the track which earned him his place on the wing. And although his heart was in the game, he wasn't all that good – not when compared to his athletic talent.

To be fair, he didn't get much opportunity to show his rugby skills. As his name became better known and once the opposition knew that the famous runner, Eric Liddell, was on the wing, he was 'a marked man'. In one game he was tackled so often, he said afterwards, that he'd seen nothing of the match. He'd spent the afternoon either face down in the mud or cleaning the mud from his eyes and mouth.

It may seem in all this time of training, racing and playing rugby, to say nothing of all the travelling involved from place to place, even country to country, that he was neglecting his studies, but he wasn't.

In his first year at University, he gained 83% in Mathematics and 94% in Chemistry. The following year he came first in his two classes and the year after he came first again with 90%.

In the summer of 1922, a few months before the family returned to China, they all went to stay at Largs. This is a beautiful seaside resort on the River Clyde at Ayrshire on the east coast of Scotland.

Even though it was holiday time there was no rest from Eric's heavy sporting schedule. Each week saw him travelling to different race meetings and one vivid memory of that holiday was when he ran in an event at Greenock. This is about fifteen miles up the coast from Largs. The rain poured down all day and the meeting was held on a saturated grass track. The athletes feet felt like lead and the water sprayed up round their legs as they ran.

Experience had shown Eric there were easier ways to dig 'starting blocks' than with the toes so he'd treated himself to an expensive, broad bladed knife. After he'd run — and won — his race, the sweat was running cold on his body, and he was so uncomfortable in his wet, clinging vest and shorts he went straight to the changing-room. He forgot all about collecting his knife from where he'd left it at the start and when he went for it later, it had gone.

By the time he set off again for Largs on the back of a friend's motorbike, he was cold, wet, tired, hungry and thoroughly fed up, but worse was to come.

Half-way there, the pillion-seat broke. Eric fell off, landing on his back in the middle of the muddy road while the unsuspecting motorcyclist rode on for about 100 yards. When he eventually realised he'd lost his passenger, he stopped and turned round to see a bedraggled Eric racing after him on foot.

As miserable as he was, to his friend's astonishment, Eric couldn't stop laughing. They managed to repair the seat with a piece of frayed string and Eric spent the rest of his soggy journey on the wobbly pillion, holding on to the string and praying it wouldn't snap.

No one could have enjoyed playing rugby and running races more than he did. But the one thing Eric didn't like was the publicity that went with it.

Wherever he raced, crowds flocked to see him and cheer him on. Once they had hopes of a future Scottish champion in Innes G Stewart. Now they had two hopefuls and the second one was Eric H Liddell.

In the excitement of a race well won or a game well played, Eric could be swept up in the excitement and applause but he didn't seem to think of it as being for him personally – more for either his team, his university or his country. Had he stopped to realise the crowd was on its feet for Eric Liddell he would have been so embarrassed he would probably have kept on running just to escape.

Whenever he spoke to anyone about some forthcoming event and who was likely to win it, he would talk about the chances of *all* the competitors. If Eric Liddell's name was mentioned he would discuss him as though he was merely another competitor whom he'd heard of but didn't actually know.

The one sad period in those first successful years was when his father's leave came to and end and the family returned to China. As it was his first leave in many years, James had been given much longer than was usual for a missionary. Naturally, they'd all enjoyed being together and had become very close again. Yet, this only made it harder to part when the time came.

With misted eyes, the two brothers stood at Waverly Station waving 'Goodbye' to their parents, sister and brother. Then, when the train was gone from sight, they turned and walked away.

James and Mary had always hoped their sons would one day return to China but now they weren't too sure. Although no one had said anything, they all sensed that Eric faced another destiny. Still, if his life was meant to follow a different course, it would have their blessing. No pressure would be put on him to become a missionary. As it was, missionaries' children rarely followed in their fathers' footsteps so James and Mary were thankful that at least one son, Robbie, was intent on doing so.

1921 had been an excellent year for Christian missionaries in China. There had been more converts than ever. More churches, schools and colleges were built and hospitals and institutions such as orphanages were opening everywhere.

1922 was even better for mission workers, especially those from Britain and Russia. All the same, life wasn't going to be easy when they returned. Because of all this success those who were opposed to Christianity were more active and an Anti-Christian Movement was set up.

This time the threat wasn't from the Boxers in their white trousers and shirts with their heads swathed in red kerchiefs. It came from the Communists who had taken over from Sun Yat Sen.

Although the Liddells had loved living at Siao Chang on China's Great Plain, after their last leave, when Robbie and Eric were left behind to attend school, they had been reposted to Peking. With time, they'd grown used to working in that lovely old city. It had changed enormously though since they first went there. The Forbidden City had been opened up to the public as a museum although there was still one closed part where the deposed Emperor lived. Now, P'u yu was a young man and had recently married, but he would go on living, almost as a prisoner, for the rest of his life in Peking under the control of the new republic.

Now, once again, James was to be re-posted – to Tientsin, a place which held horrific memories for Mary. Her one happiness there had been the birth of their second son, Eric. She had never dreamed that the time would come when she would live there again. Nevertheless, missionaries were always ready to accept whatever duty was given them.

They settled down to the long journey ahead of them, wondering what their future years in China would bring and also worrying about Eric's future. Robbie would be with them in a year's time but when would they ever see Eric again?

6: Eric Liddell, Evangelist

The boys had no family home to return to now and they felt utterly lost.

They'd arranged to go and live in George Square at the Edinburgh Medical Missionary Society Hostel. It sounded quite forbidding after the easy-going atmosphere of home with all its warmth and love that they'd known for the past two years. There was however one consolation – they had each other's company – at least for another year.

Despite Eric's strong team spirit and the fact that he was very popular with lots of friends, he was still a bit of a loner. And he much preferred having his brother's company to anyone else's.

However, when they moved into the hostel it was to discover a home as happy as the one they'd just lost.

About twelve students lived there and the warden, Dr Lachlan Taylor, his wife and daughter were a jolly group. Their one aim was to make their boarders feel a part of the family.

Unlike Eric, Robbie was dark like his parents and as tall as James and his father before him. Eric was rather short. He had long, narrow features which ended in a dimple at his chin and even in his early twenties, his fair hair was beginning to recede from his forehead. His mother blamed it on all the hot showers he took after playing rugby or racing. This balding didn't age Eric in the way it does with most men. His sense of fun always made him appear to be younger than his years.

Mrs Taylor, the warden's wife, liked both brothers. But Eric, with his slow speech and quiet ways, appealed to her especially. Cooking was her greatest pride. She loved to see all the young men in her charge devouring the delicious food set before them. Underlying Eric's twinkling blue eyes and wide grin, she sensed the shyness that was there. And because he *never* asked for a second helping at the table, she was convinced it was because he was so shy. This made her give him extra portions on his plate which he felt obliged to eat.

What Mrs Taylor didn't realise was that this was the wrong way to feed an athlete. One day after a filling meal of pies and plum pudding – of which Eric ate little – the others tried to explain it was because he was racing later that afternoon. Mrs Taylor reasoned that in that case, he should *eat more* to sustain his strength, and Eric was too polite to refuse.

Oddly enough, on that day he ran one of the fastest races of his life.

In the early months of 1922 a big Christian Evangelistic campaign had started in Scotland.

It covered all denominations and its main appeal lay in having young people conducting the meetings. Among them were College and University students as well as young men who had survived the Great War. All were willing to give up their spare time to travel the country, trying to urge people back into the churches and into the arms of Christ.

Robbie Liddell, or Bob as his friends called him, had joined the crusade right at the beginning but Eric hadn't shown much interest.

No one was sure exactly how he did feel about religion, the church or God Himself. It was obvious that he lived a good Christian life, quietly following the rules without question. But he certainly never spoke on the subject.

In groups of twelve, the University students travelled to speak in various towns where they had been invited. They were not necessarily Divinity or Theology students. Some were reading Science, Law, Medicine, the Arts and other unrelated subjects.

At each town, they would camp and cater for themselves in church halls for about a week at a time. At the end of every day, they would all cluster around the coke-boiler and discuss the day's successes – or failures. Then they would go on to suggest ways of improving their approach or the campaign in general.

In most places they had an excellent response. But in others, mainly the big industrial towns and cities, the mission wasn't going quite as well as they'd hoped. Women, children and the elderly flocked to the meetings but they were usually regular churchgoers already.

It was the non-churchgoers the evangelists were aiming at and these were almost always the working men. They believed there were more manly things to do, such as drinking, gambling, even brawling and, of course, going to football matches every Saturday.

When a group of Glasgow students moved into Armadale, a large industrial town situated half-way between Glasgow and Edinburgh, they sensed they would be faced with the now-familiar situation.

All one evening they sat and pondered on the problem. What could they do to get the men's interest? There was a half-day holiday coming in the middle of the following week. And not being a Saturday, the men they needed to attract would be spending the day in the pub.

'Suppose *we* challenge the locals to a match. Wouldn't that appeal to them?' asked one.

This was the best idea anyone had thought of and the rest set to planning and publicising it at once.

They were amazed at how many attended the football match and they were secretly delighted when their own students team won five to two against the locals.

'That says something for being on the Lord's side,' one joked.

But facing facts; one solitary football match added up to *one* solitary success. It hadn't even touched on what they were there for – to get those men into the church. Something more needed to be done, and quickly before the match was forgotten and the interest faded.

Then David Thomson, a theology student from Glasgow, thought of Eric Liddell, the Edinburgh University student and famous sportsman.

His brother, Bob, had been on several 'crusades' with David Thomson. And David knew his father was an ordained church minister and a missionary in China and that his brother was the famous athlete. Still, he didn't know Eric personally or know anything about his religious beliefs. What he was sure of was that Eric Liddell's presence would attract a crowd from anywhere and to anything. If they could get him to come then who better to give a talk to these poor people – *spiritually* poor when they didn't know or even want to know the Lord.

Everyone in the church hall that night thought that David (or DP as they all called him) had a brilliant idea. If the great Eric Liddell agreed to come they would arrange to hold a meeting for men only in Armadale Town Hall and have him as their guest speaker.

As DP had been the one to suggest it, he offered to go himself the very next morning and ask him.

Short of money, he hitched a lift to Edinburgh on a smelly petrol lorry and went to the Mission Hostel where he knew the brothers were living.

He asked to speak to Bob first because they knew each

other so well. But when he asked him if Eric would help with their campaign, Bob said, 'Oh, I think you'd better ask him yourself.'

When he went away to bring his brother, DP began to doubt if his idea had been such a good one. Bob didn't sound very confident of Eric agreeing.

Minutes later Eric came into the room and walked forward, proffering his hand. DP had never imagined he would ever shake hands with this famous man and his words stuck in his throat. However could he have thought *he* would help in their humble crusade?

Quickly and anxiously he explained his visit while Eric listened carefully without interrupting. When DP finished speaking he felt his anxiety was justified as a silence fell on the room and Eric hung his head.

He thought deeply for a minute then he looked up and gave that lovely smile that endeared him to everyone. 'All right. I'll come,' he said.

DP sighed with relief and thanked him then he hastened back to Armadale with the good news.

Neither he nor Eric were aware of how those few minutes and that simple request would change Eric's entire life.

Robbie went with him to Armadale for the meeting and at precisely 9 o'clock, on the 6th April, 1923 in the Town Hall, Robert Victor Liddell officially opened the meeting. There were about eighty in the audience. Not a great number but more than would have attended without knowing who the guest was to be.

After saying a few words of welcome, Robbie introduced his brother then took some steps back and sat down.

The audience sat in silence, waiting. They all knew of Eric Liddell, the international rugby player and best athlete Scotland had ever known. But of Eric Liddell, the *man* they knew nothing.

As for Eric himself, well, he could feel confident on the rugby pitch or the running track. There he knew what he was doing. But could he match that skill as a public speaker, he wondered? He hated the 'limelight' and always tried to avoid having interviews with reporters or posing for photographs in newspapers and magazines.

Shyly, he stepped forward and for a few seconds he surveyed his waiting audience, then he began.

There was no lecturing, no fist thumping on the table, no wagging or pointing finger to stress his meaning, no raised voice to impress on their ears what he thought they should be doing.

In fact, it wasn't a speech at all. More of a quiet chat as, in his slow, clear words Eric, for the first time in his life told the world what God meant to him. He spoke of the strength he felt within himself from the sure knowledge of God's love and support. Of how he never questioned anything that happened either to himself or to others. He didn't need explanations from God. He simply believed in Him and accepted whatever came.

The people were enthralled and through his genuine humility they stopped thinking of him as the famous man they'd come to see.

When he'd finished, DP stepped forward, thanked him then said a few words of his own before closing the meeting.

The following morning, *every newspaper in Scotland* reported that Eric Liddell had taken part in an evangelical meeting at Armadale the previous evening.

A week later, Eric was speaking at another meeting in Rutherglen, a town just outside of Glasgow. There the audience numbered six hundred.

Suddenly, something new and wonderful had entered Eric's life.

Until then it had never occurred to him to speak openly

of his faith. He had lived with it all his life. It was as natural as eating, bathing, sleeping and breathing. Who went about informing people they did those things? And anyway, he'd always thought it was a private matter between himself and God. But now, he wanted to carry the love of the Lord into every living soul.

He vowed to go on the 'crusades' as often as possible and from then on, he showed no reserve in talking of his faith – of how he was totally committed to God – of how *God* was totally committed to everybody in the world. All the Lord asked was that they let him into their lives and their hearts.

Eric often thanked David Thomson for travelling to Edinburgh on that morning to seek his assistance. For his part, David never ceased to thank God for introducing him to such a man as Eric Liddell. Until they met, he had never dreamed any mortal could be so good. If everyone's nickname for David was DP, then his special name for Eric was always 'Sir Galahad'. No man was more worthy of the title.

The two became lifelong friends. Eric looked upon DP almost as a brother. They campaigned together in England as well as Scotland and wherever Eric appeared, people flocked to hear him. It was becoming increasingly clear too that they weren't coming to see the celebrated sportsman. Eric was the man who brought God to thousands.

No one likes to be lectured or preached at nor feel they are being told how to live their lives. Therefore, perhaps it was Eric's simple approach to them that made him so successful. He related God to every single aspect and second of his own life. Far from ordering people to live better lives, he was saying he hoped they would share and enjoy God's love with him.

He confided in them how, each morning, he set aside some

time to meditate and pray or read some passage from the Bible. This was his special time with God which helped him to plan his entire day. And if circumstances sometimes forced him to miss that time with his maker, he felt at odds with the world and everyone in it for the rest of that day. It was as if he was 'out of tune' with God himself.

Throughout the United Kingdom, Eric was admired for his evangelistic work. But he did have some critics. Those who had said he wasn't a good rugby player were now saying that, giving so much time to his work, he would neglect his obligations to sport. Just at a time when Scotland was glowing with pride over her new champion.

But they were wrong. The two went together. Eric was running *for* Scotland and he was running *with* the Lord.

Now he had openly admitted his deep faith, his feet had wings. Instead of a decline in his running, he improved with every race.

Each weekend he was campaigning somewhere as well as racing. During the week he was getting on with his studies. All this was enough to drain any man but Eric felt fitter and happier than at any other time in his life.

In Scotland he was winning every race including the 100 and 220 yards in the SAAA (Scottish Amateur Athletic Association) Championships. Still, as his times weren't exceptional, his critics then said he couldn't run. To be fair, they were really saying, with his awkward style he shouldn't be able to run—much less keep winning. When one asked him how he managed to find the tape when he didn't even look where he was going, Eric replied 'The Lord guides me.'

When the time came for the AAA Championships in England, some of the press said that, because of his poor times, it seemed hardly worthwhile spending £5 on sending him to London to take part. And although his fame as a sportsman and evangelist had spread all over Britain, he had *never* run a race in London.

But Eric and his trainer showed more faith than the press or any other doubter. And anyway, Eric could never resist a challenge. Together they set off for Stamford Bridge, London.

It was a hot summer and Eric was happy with such weather. It relaxes the muscles, making them loose and this was ideal for his short-distance racing.

At the stadium in Stamford Bridge, all eyes were on the young Scot. The spectators were then highly surprised when, at the beginning of his first race, Eric walked along the line of contestants, shaking hands with each one and expressing his good wishes for their success. He didn't wish them 'Good Luck!' Luck was something he didn't believe in. It would be the Lord who decided which one would win.

After losing his knife at Greenock, he'd started to use a trowel. After the handshaking and well wishing, he then offered to lend his trowel to those who were still digging their 'starting blocks' with their toes.

Neither the crowd nor the competitors had ever experienced such sportsmanship. Some were in open-mouthed admiration. Many were greatly amused.

To disprove all doubts, Eric won the 220 yards in 21.6 seconds. He then won the 100 yards in 9.7 seconds, a new record for the whole of Britain. It was thirty-five years before it was broken.

But Eric's wins were not easy. On the Friday, July 6th, 1923 the sun was burning down and he had to run two first heats; one for the 100, another for the 220 yards sprint.

The following day, Saturday, he ran four times. Twice in the second heats, at half past two and ten past three. These were followed almost immediately by the finals which were run at twenty minutes to four and at five past four. He won

73

all six races and for his outstanding performance that day he was awarded the Harvey Cup as best champion of the year.

This was some achievement but if he could give a similar performance the following week there would be no doubt in anyone's mind where Eric Liddell would be competing a year later.

The Olympic Games were to take place in Paris, July, 1924. Until that Saturday only one had been seriously considered for the British team. That was Harold Abrahams.

He was a student at Cambridge University in England. He came from a German/Jewish family and all his life he had been fighting racial prejudice. His ambition was to overcome that prejudice by becoming a renowned athlete and running for England, his family's adopted country.

The following week's race meeting was at Stoke-on-Trent. It was the Triangular International Contest between England, Scotland and Ireland and Eric knew the sort of opponent he faced in Harold Abrahams. He really looked forward to meeting him though because Eric always loved a challenge.

Unfortunately, they didn't compete against each aother. When Eric arrived at Stoke-on-Trent he was told that Harold had a severe throat infection and couldn't run. He would have to content himself with being a spectator. They were actually introduced to each other at that meeting and became very good friends.

Eric wasn't particularly worried about the 100 or 220 yards. They were his ideal distances. The 440 yards – the quarter mile – wasn't. He'd rarely entered for that distance and had never run it in a Scottish Championship. Nor had he done any training for it at Stoke.

There was just one spark of hope at the back of his mind. It was after eating Mrs Taylor's pies and pudding in Edinburgh that he ran his fastest ever quarter mile. But that had only been a *local* contest. Still, at Stoke he wouldn't be eating pies or puddings so he stood a slight chance.

But disaster struck. The race started on the bend with Eric on the inside. The starting pistol sounded and everyone got off to a good start – for the first three strides.

Then, Gillies, one of the England runners, tripped and crashed into Eric sending him stumbling from the track on to the grass verge at the side. The crowd gasped in horror. Eric seemed stunned. Bitterly disappointed and sure of disqualification – although it had clearly been an accident – he came to a halt. Then he noticed the officials frantically signalling to him. For a moment he tried to make out what they were saying.

Suddenly he understood. They were telling him to carry on. But Eric knew it wasn't possible to catch up. His leading opponents were already twenty yards ahead. Yet, as if spurred on by some superior force, the plucky athlete leapt back on to the track. Again the crowd gasped as he thundered along. Everyone knew, no one could make up that distance.

Still, he went on and on and on. Spectators gaped wide eyed. Their hearts pumping as fast as his own.

When the runners reached the home stretch, Eric Liddell had not only caught them up – he was lying *fourth*, a mere ten yards behind Gillies. At that point his strength visibly began to ebb away and it was obvious he was about to collapse. He set his teeth hard and from somewhere deep inside came some super-human energy. Instead of crumpling to the ground, he carried on. He fought for breath. His knees came up ever higher and his fists thumped out at the air as though trying to cut a way through it. In a flash he was running third, second, then finally he shot ahead of Gillies to win the race by *two yards*.

The onlookers were near hysterics. They rose to their feet

as one person, clapping and cheering for Eric Liddell, a man who had achieved the impossible in the face of absolute defeat.

Not least among his admirers were Gillies himself and the one who should have been there in the race, Harold Abrahams.

People were commenting about the strange expression on his face as he raced to the finish and they felt honoured to have been present to witness such an outstanding victory – an impossible victory. That expression was *faith*.

At the tape, Eric did collapse and was carried away on a stretcher. Someone offered brandy to help bring him round but Eric managed to open his eyes and murmur, 'No thanks, I'll just have a drop of strong tea.'

With his efforts he'd damaged muscle tissue in his thighs and his head was spinning and throbbing for days from the fatigue.

When he was asked later how he'd managed to win, he replied, 'The first half I ran as fast as I could. The second half I ran faster with God's help.'

That afternoon, he'd easily won the 100 and 220 yards but it was his valiant performance in the quarter mile which had everyone talking and had all his press critics reporting on. This and the fact that, for the first and last time, one athlete won all three short-distance International races on the one afternoon, ensured that Eric Liddell would be in the British Olympic team the following year in Paris.

He would be entered for the 200 metres and the 100 metres (in Europe the distances were measured in metres but were almost the equivalent of our 220 and 100 yards). Eric was reigning British Champion for the 100 which also happened to be his favourite race and it was the most sought after win of the Olympic Games. Because of all this, he desperately wanted to run that race for Britain in Paris.

Still, there was a long time to go before then. First there was the Inter Varsity Sports Meeting at which he again won the 100, 220 and 440 yards races and broke all three records. The 440 yards record went unbroken for a further thirty-four years.

After this, he was headed for America where a whole string of misfortunes awaited him. Well, really they began before he even got there.

As the liner *Berengaria* set sail from England's shores, he realised he'd left half of his luggage behind .... The following day, Eric was wishing *he'd* been left behind. As a little boy he'd spent six weeks sailing from China to Britain but that had been a long time ago. This time he was terribly seasick and it lasted for most of the Atlantic crossing.

On arrival, there were hordes of reporters and photographers all so eager for interviews and press photos it was impossible to leave the ship.

During that visit, his racing wasn't up to standard either. If he ran the best race of his life at Stoke-on-Trent, he ran the worst one at a big athletic meeting in Philadelphia. In his best distance, the 100 yards, the great Eric Liddell whom everyone was eager to see, came fourth although, in truth, there were only a matter of three inches between all first four places.

He wasn't sorry when it was time to leave America and he looked forward so much to returning to Britain, especially to Edinburgh. But there was more upset. On arriving back he learned that the two suitcases he'd filled with souvenirs and gifts for everyone were missing.

As if that wasn't enough, Robbie told him he would be leaving for China within a short time. He was now qualified and as Dr Robert Victor Liddell, he wanted to take his place in a hospital close to his parents.

Fortunately, Eric had all the winter and the following

spring to recover from his unhappy American trip and the loss of his brother before embarking on his greatest ordeal of all, preparing for the 1924 Olympic Games in France.

After Robbie left for China, Eric, for the first time in his life, felt entirely alone. He had his special friend, DP but they were miles apart because DP was still at Glasgow University. And anyway, his home was at Crieff in Perthshire, quite a distance from Edinburgh.

There were the Taylors and Eric was very fond of them. But, of course, their home was always full of students. Even in their midst Eric could be lonely. The busy life he led was a great help at that time.

There was his BSc to work for. Many evangelism campaigns were organised and not only in Scotland. More and more the students were travelling into England. Eric often wondered if the Lord had guided him into that work as a comfort when his earthly family were out of reach.

By now he had retired from rugby to concentrate more on his athletics – training as much for his own fitness as for the forthcoming Olympics.

7: Olympic Gold

The first Olympic Games on record were held at Olympia, Greece in 176 BC. They were partly to entertain the people and, to honour the twelve gods who lived on Mount Olympus, the greatest of which was Zeus.

Only the cream of the nation's youth could take part and this did *not* include females.

Originally, the Games lasted for one day only and consisted of running and wrestling. Later, other sports such as boxing, javelin and discus throwing, horse racing and chariot races were added. In time the arts – dancing, music, poetry and literature were introduced and eventually the Games had to be extended to a five day-event to accommodate all these additions.

In Greece a group of four years is an Olympiad, called thus because the games were held at four-yearly intervals. And to this day, that same rule applies. The Olympics always began with sacrifices to the gods – one rule which happily no longer applies. After the sacrifices the contestants would stand in front of a statue of Zeus to take a solemn oath of honesty and fairness.

Prizes at the ancient Games were olive leaf crowns, of no monetary value at all. Yet, an Olympic winner valued that crown above all he owned. Once crowned, he would be carried shoulder high in great triumph back to his native city or village. There, the victor wouldn't be expected to enter through the gate. He was so important a personage that a special opening would be made in the wall through which he could be carried. At home he would be treated like an Emperor.

Sadly it was the Emperor, Theodoseus I, who abolished the Games. It was one of his first acts when he came to the throne in AD 393. No one was sure why he disapproved of them and, naturally, no one questions an Emperor.

Fifteen hundred years went by before they were re-introduced thanks to a French Baron, Pierre de Courbetin. He believed in the principles of honesty and fairness and in the friendly competition of sport. He believed in something else too. It shouldn't be exclusive to one nation. Sport should be a worldwide concern.

The first of the modern Olympic Games were played in 1896 at Athens, the capital city of Greece, their country of origin.

From then on, with the exception of the two World Wars, they have been held every four years as an international event and each Olympics has a different host country. 1912 saw women enter for the first time and 1924 saw the start of the winter Olympics. 1924 was also the year Eric Liddell was chosen to take a place in the British team in July of that year in Paris.

As the winter of that year drew to a close and spring began to creep in, excitement bubbled among all those chosen to represent their country. The timetable of events was due out at any time and everyone was eager to know on what particular day and at what time of the day he or she would be competing.

That day came and Eric was as eager as anyone to read it. But when he did he was completely astounded for it showed something he'd never given a moment's thought to.

His race, the 100 metres, was to have its first heats run

on a *Sunday*. And the Sabbath was a day to be devoted to God, not sport.

Without a moment's hesitation but with sadness in his voice Eric quietly said, 'I'm not running.'

Everyone turned to stare at him, disbelief all over their faces. Then he pointed out the date and time on the paper.

When Eric said something, he meant it. These weren't the words of an impetuous young man, spoken in a second's thoughtlessness only to be regretted afterwards.

He wasn't running. It was as simple as that and there was no point in arguing with him.

When he told the athletic authorities in Britain, instead of trying to cajole or abuse him for his beliefs, they immediately contacted the Olympic officials. Could they possible rearrange the dates, they asked? But they refused. No one on the continent could understand why Eric was making such a fuss. Yet, Eric wasn't making any fuss. Everyone else was.

Why couldn't he run on Sunday and dedicate the race to God, some asked?

Others said he was a traitor to his country, refusing to run for Scotland simply because the chosen day didn't suit him. He was their best, probably only, hope of gaining a much coveted Olympic gold medal. No Briton had won a gold in the 100 metres since the Games were revived in 1896.

But nothing that anyone or any newspaper said could induce Eric to change his mind. Years later he admitted that it had upset him a lot. He was no traitor to his country. He was just refusing to betray his religious beliefs – and God came first.

Many athletes admired him for sticking to those beliefs. There were also many athletes who were pleased to learn that their greatest rival, already recognised as one of the fastest-ever men in the world, was dropping out.

As if Eric hadn't been disappointed enough, when the times for the 4×400 and 4×100 metre relays came out, it was revealed they too were being run on a Sunday. Naturally, he refused to run in those as well.

The authorities were very embarrassed by all this and felt they must put him in some event as he was part of the team. He wasn't their greatest hope when it came to the 200 and 400 metres. But now he was asked to put in some extra training for them and Eric was happy to do so.

When news of all this trouble reached China, Eric's family was very distressed for his sake. Yet, at the same time, they were immensely proud of him. For years, they'd accepted that he was lost to them as far as mission work in China was concerned. They knew all about his evangelical campaigning. Robbie had given them all the details on that. But they also knew that his sporting activities shared exactly the same amount of time as the campaigns.

Now, with this latest development, it seemed Eric's choice had been made. God meant more to him than a gold medal. All the same, he hadn't yet taken part in the Paris Olympics. They could make a difference in his attitude, if not toward the Lord, to his career.

While Eric was facing all this trouble in Scotland, his family was coping with the outbreak of yet another Civil War in China. Government officials were constantly being replaced by others until no one knew who was in charge or of what. Chaos reigned as the entire country was brought to a standstill through lack of order.

Skirmishes and heavy battles resulted in much bloodshed and nature seemed to be waging war against China too. Floods, and famines saw people homeless. There was disease and of course all this brought more deaths.

It was at this time that Eric applied for a teaching post at the Anglo-Chinese College in Tientsin – the college which had its foundations laid in the days following the Boxer uprising and Eric's own birth in the city. It was also the place from which all those magazines had come that Robbie and Eric read so avidly when they were children at Eltham. And more recently, Tientsin had become the home of the Liddell family.

He knew there would be a long wait before he heard if he'd been given the teaching post, or even been considered for it. But there was too much to do for him to brood on the outcome of his application.

In June, a month before he was to leave for Paris, Eric ran in the Scottish AAA Championships at Hampden Park, Glasgow. He won the 100, 220 and 440 yards races. Yet, his times were so poor, the spectators thought perhaps Scotland had lost nothing when he dropped out of the Olympics.

The same people were even more convinced two weeks later when they again met at Hampden Park for the Scottish Inter-Varsity sports and, once again, his times were disappointing.

That crowd was witness to the side of Eric Liddell which surpassed any sporting victory.

One of the rival students from Aberdeen University was sitting on the grass beside the track waiting to run in the final of the relay race. There was a coolish breeze blowing and Eric was shocked to see that this rival was wearing only a thin vest and shorts. He strode up to him and gazed down for a moment. Then the Edinburgh student took off his own blue uniform blazer and stooped to drape it round the athlete's bare shoulders. A warm smile spread across his face and he murmured, 'You must take care not to catch cold.'

Today, the Olympic Games are big business with world-wide TV coverage, sponsors, interviews and videos all playing their part. The competitors themselves undergo almost non-stop training, dieting, medical checks, massage and work-outs. In 1924, it was still very amateurish and the whole thing was for pleasure – with a ration of national pride added.

Nearly all the competitors were University students and the 1924 Olympic Games were the first to see some of them being subsidised – given financial assistance. Until then, athletes went at their own expense. It was never a simple question of 'Who was the most promising?' but 'Who could afford to go?' Without the subsidy, Eric most certainly couldn't have gone.

The wealthiest countries of the world were able to give more support to their athletes than other countries. America for instance, sent her Olympic team on *two* ships – a battleship and the liner *America*. On the luxurious liner, a 200 metre cork track had been laid out over one of her decks. This enabled the athletes to practice during the long Atlantic voyage to Europe.

When all the contestants arrived in Paris they had to *hitch* lifts to get to the Colombe Stadium. There was no official transport laid on for them and wealthy spectators were paying more than double the taxi fares to the stadium. This meant there were no taxis left available for the competitors.

On the day before the Games opened, led by their captain, the British team marched up the Champs Elysées to the Arc de Triomph. Ahead of them went the Band of the Queen's Own Cameron Highlanders playing a Scottish lament, The Flowers of the Forest. At the Arc de Triomph, His Royal Highness, The Prince of Wales, who later became King Edward VIII, placed a wreath on the tomb of the Unknown Warrior.

It was a sombre incident and as the mournful dirge played on, they all hoped it wasn't an indication of what lay ahead in the next few days.

Saturday, July 5th, 1924, was the day for the 8th Olympiad of modern times to begin. After the first Games were played in Greece in 1896, as a tribute to the French Baron who revived them, the second Olympics were staged in Paris. Now twenty years later, they were in Paris again. It was a day so hot that people were fainting before the Games had even started.

Compared to the first Olympics when thirteen countries took part, this time there were forty-five countries and the stadium was filled with 60,000 onlookers.

Four French Military bands played as the first team – from South Africa – marched through the Marathon . Gate and the spectacle began.

Amid the waving and cheering there came the skirl of the pipes and the Queen's Cameron Highlanders emerged from the gateway. They were an impressive sight in their swinging kilts and bearskin headdress. For a moment the crowd seemed mesmerised at the sight and sound but when the team from Great Britain came marching in behind the band, the cheers rang out even louder.

The British women wore cream, pleated skirts. The men were in cream trousers. All had on blue blazers and white straw hats. Proudly they marched past the podium where the President of France stood alongside the ageing Baron Pierre de Courbetin.

There were princes, ambassadors and nobility from all over the world including our own Prince of Wales and his young brother, Prince George, later to become the Duke of Gloucester.

Nation after nation marched in behind their flag and the bands played on, their sound almost drowned by the cheering crowd. America's team numbered 400. Haiti had but one competitor.

Finally, the forty-five countries were assembled and the

1924 Olympic Games were officially opened by the Baron who had revived the Games just twenty-eight years before.

When he finished his short speech, the bands all played La Marseillaise – France's national anthem – as the five ringed Olympic flag was raised to the top of the giant flagpole. Then cannons roared to tell all of Paris the Games were about to begin.

The Olympic relay torch wasn't a part of the ceremony in those days but thousands of pigeons were released to wing their way over the entire country with the good news.

After this, the Olympic Oath was recited and then the four thousand competitors, representing their forty-five nations, filed out of the arena again to more wild cheering and waving.

The 8th Olympiad had begun.

All this while, Eric was coming under a lot of pressure to run in the 100 metres. Really it hadn't stopped from that day months earlier when he'd said he wouldn't run. But once in Paris the criticism began to hurt more.

The newspapers were making snide remarks and although Eric wasn't referred to by name, everyone knew who the press was getting at.

At the opening celebrations, just after the team left the arena, one of Britain's leading noblemen went to give them his good wishes.

'To play the game is the only thing in life that matters,' he said.

Eric felt these words were being directed towards him and in a way he agreed with them. But 'playing the game' could mean many things. To him it meant sticking to the rules and he was doing just that – sticking to the rules by which he lived his life.

His great comfort through those trying moments was to recite to himself a favourite Bible quotation 'Whosoever believeth in me shall not be ashamed'.

Eric went to see Harold Abrahams, Britain's remaining

hope for a medal in the 100 metres and he wished him well. As a Jew, Harold's Sabbath was Saturday and Eric respected this. He understood that it was as right for Harold to run on a Sunday as it would have been wrong for himself.

Sunday, July 6th saw the young Cambridge University student Abrahams lined up for the 100 metres preliminary heat. At the same time, Eric Liddell was addressing a congregation in the Scots Kirk (church) on the other side of Paris.

Harold came through both heats. The following day he was all set for the semi-final and among the watchers was Eric to cheer him on to victory. Then came the final and it was a great victory for Harold who reached the tape in 10.6 seconds. The stadium erupted in loud applause. No European had ever won a gold medal in that event and it would be fifty six years before one won it again.

Deep inside, Eric must have felt a tinge of regret – but there wasn't an element of envy in him. He was elated for Harold's success.

Now he felt free of the criticism too and was able to concentrate on his own two events.

The heats for the 200 metre race were held on the Tuesday. Both Eric and Harold qualified in each for a place in the final the next day.

Wednesday was another searingly hot day; the day of the 200 metre final in which Eric was lined up alongside Harold Abrahams and four Americans. Both British boys got off to a good start but first one then the other fell behind. Two of the Americans reached the tape first to take a gold and a silver medal. Eric came third and Harold ran sixth in last place.

This may seem disastrous, yet it was really a success for Eric. Scotland had never won a bronze for the 200 metre race. And the whole of Britain had never achieved anything better than third place and a bronze medal.

Still this victory failed to raise anyone's expectations for the 400 metres. Britain only had one hope for that race, Guy Butler. Guy had come second to win a silver in the 400 metres at Antwerp in Belgium four years earlier in the 1920 Olympics. But now that hope was dimmed. He had recently injured his leg and with a heavily bandaged thigh he wasn't able to crouch for the off. Starting from a standing position would surely lose the race for him although he was determined to run his best.

As for Eric, well, declining to run in the 100 metres had ruined his only chance for a gold. No one supposed a 100 or 200 metre runner would have anything like the necessary qualities for the 400 metres; or *vice versa*. They were two entirely different races calling for completely different abilities.

But when it came to Thursday and the 400 metre heats, Eric didn't do too badly. He didn't shine either even though his time improved in each heat. It was better still the next day in the semi-final. Still, he only managed to qualify. On the previous day, in one heat, Imbach of Switzerland actually broke the world record when he ran the distance in 48 seconds.

On the Friday which saw the semi-final and the final, the stifling, airless atmosphere was beginning to affect everyone. Even some of the contestants were sick from the sun beating down on them, morning till night. Fortunately, the finals were to be run at 7 o'clock in the evening. It would only be slightly cooler then but it was welcome.

There were six finalists: two Americans, one Canadian, Imbach of Switzerland and the two British boys, Guy Butler and Eric Liddell.

As usual, Eric went along the line shaking the competitors' hands and giving them his best wishes. This was a ritual the international crowd had begun to look for and still thought it strange to see one sportsman wishing well for his rivals – but they didn't know Eric the man.

Everyone there had a feeling of respect for Guy Butler. It took a stout heart to enter a race which he knew was lost to him before he started. The entire crowd was quite resigned to the fact that America would take the gold and possibly the silver. The big question in their minds was, who of the remaining four would take the bronze?

In the last few moments before the off, as the athletes were warming up, without any warning, a mighty sound filled the enormous arena. The pipes and drums of the Queens Own Cameron Highlanders had struck up with 'The Campbells Are Coming'.

The British team organiser, Sir Philip Christison, sensed some despondency among the British supporters and he thought some rousing music would cheer them up. Maybe it would spur Eric Liddell on too. After all, he was a Scot and the skirl of the pipes would surely send the blood racing through his veins – just at a time when it was most needed.

Round and round the band marched whilst the competitors waited. Eventually, the music faded. A tense silence returned only to be shattered by the sharp crack of the starting pistol and Eric was off.

No one could believe what they were seeing. Right from the start he leapt into a three metre lead. On he went with that awful running style of his. He resembled a feeble swimmer, out of his depth and struggling for air; thrashing out with his arms and legs.

Everyone knew he couldn't keep up that pace. A 100 metre man couldn't do what he was doing. Still, he pounded on. Guy Butler was running his heart out too. For a while the crowd seemed hypnotised. Then, the expected occurred. Fitch, one of the Americans, overtook Butler to sprint closer and closer to Eric who was still in the lead. But again, the unexpected happened. Eric began to run *even faster*.

Closer and closer he drew to the tape – without seeing it. His head was right back on his shoulders and his eyes were looking up to heaven. From out of nowhere it seemed, hosts of British Union Jacks appeared amongst the onlookers to wave him on to victory.

Suddenly, after what seemed miles, the 400 metre race was over. Eric Liddell reached the tape a full *five metres* ahead of Fitch with the injured Guy Butler sprinting into third place to take a bronze.

The crowd's roar could be heard all over Paris. Then, in a brief spell of quiet, a voice boomed out over the speaker to announce that Eric had run the race in a new world record time of 47·6 seconds. This time it seemed as though the cheers would be heard across the channel in Britain.

Amid the cheers, laughter and tears of elation, the mighty Union Jack was hoisted into the air. Second came the Stars and Stripes for Fitch, winner of the silver followed by a third Union Jack for Guy Butler's bronze medal.

Bands played. People waved, clapped, sang and cheered as Eric received his gold medal. He was physically drained but God had carried him along on winged feet. He felt nothing for himself but his heart was filled with national pride at winning the much coveted gold for his country. He accepted his medal with his usual humility then he calmly walked away to the stairs leading to the dressing-rooms. There he showered, dressed, then left to keep an important appointment back in his hotel room.

He had been invited to give an address at the Scots Kirk again the following Sunday and with preparing for his race, he hadn't had the time to prepare his address. Now it was the most important item in his mind.

General Sir Philip Christison was confident the stirring effect of the pipes and drums had spurred the 22-year-old Scot to victory that day. But Eric knew it was something quite different. It was all due to a few simple words written on a scrap of paper.

In the days leading up to his races, the masseur officially assigned to care for the British team had come to know Eric very well and he liked him immensely.

With Tom McKerchar, Eric's regular trainer and masseur, he had pummelled, slapped and rubbed the famous body every day ensuring the muscles were as pliable, soft and supple as they would ever be. Tom had worked on Eric's right side, the official masseur had taken his left. Feeling that strong heart bump, bumping away under his palms, he'd sensed there was something superior; something quite apart from anything he'd experienced with other athletes. He felt privileged to manipulate such powerful flesh.

It was some time before he was aware of what that superiority was. It wasn't just life, the gift of God he felt pounding away under his hand. It wasn't flesh but the man's spirit. Eric Liddell was so true and sincere a man that his goodness radiated and rippled from him to touch all who came close to him. Yet, there he would lie in meek silence as the hurtful massage went on and on. When it was finished he would give that beaming smile and a word of thanks that reflected his very soul.

Now the masseur understood why Eric hadn't been able to run in the 100 metres on a Sunday. A lesser man could have been swayed by the majority. Not this man. It took courage of a special sort for one so popular, so well loved and on whom so many depended to refuse what they wanted in order to do what he believed was right. But, oh, how he wished Eric Liddell would achieve victory that day in the 400 metres.

To try in some small way to show the athlete how much he admired him, as Eric was leaving his hotel that morning for the Colombes Stadium, the masseur came up to him and pressed a piece of folded paper into his hand.

Eric glanced at it, smiled and said, 'Thank you. I'll read it when I get to the Stadium.'

He had no idea what he was thanking him for but that was Eric's way. Later, in one of the few quiet times of that day, he unfolded the paper and read 'In the old book it says "He that honours me I will honour". Wishing you the best of success always.'

Eric read it again later that evening and remembered those other words 'Whosoever believeth in me shall not be ashamed'.

The following day he was being hailed by everyone – even his press critics – as the 'greatest quarter miler ever'.

No longer was he a traitor to his country. He was Scotland's hero and being likened to Bruce, Rob Roy and Wallace.

Eric viewed this change of heart with part amusement, part disinterest.

For the 1924 Olympic Games a motto had been especially created. It was 'Citius, Altius, Fortius' meaning 'Faster, Higher, Stronger' and it could apply to no competitor more than to Eric Liddell.

8: Going Home

In Paris the following Sunday, the Scots Kirk was packed with Olympic competitors and those who had travelled to Paris to watch the spectacular Games. There were also many whose task it was to ensure everything went smoothly; trainers, organisers, musicians and clerical workers. They came from all denominations, but now they had come to listen to a young man who was inviting them to join him in something much more glorious – the Kingdom of God.

A few days later Eric was travelling back to Britain, but not to a peaceful homecoming. At Victoria Station in London he was besieged by a mass of people all eager to welcome their hero. He was lifted off his feet and carried shoulder high from the station.

The modest athlete laughed and readily fell in with the festivities, rejoicing in the happiness of all around him.

By the Thursday, he was back in his beautiful Edinburgh for this was his graduation day, July, 17th 1924.

The splendour of the McEwan Hall was the setting for the graduation ceremony. It was a fitting place. For many of the graduates, this would be the most important and memorable day of their lives. Over their heads was the impressive dome with its magnificently hued figures of the Science and Art worlds standing out against a glittering gold background.

Finally, when all were gathered, the graduation ceremony

began. As each name was called out, the graduates stepped up to receive their degrees from the principal and vice-chancellor, Sir Alfred Ewing, who stood on the impressive staging which was flanked by enormous fresco panels.

Eric Liddell, BSc, would be his full title from now on, and he had earned it but, all the same, he was slightly downcast in the moments before his name was called out. If only his family could have been present, he thought, but there wasn't even Robbie now and Eric had been there for *his* graduation.

Wave after wave of applause resounded through the great hall as each student walked up to the principal. Then it was Eric's turn. To his surprise, everyone rose to their feet, cheering and clapping. The new BSc was astounded as it went on and on. Time and time again, Sir Alfred Ewing called for silence while he made a speech in honour of the Olympic Champion. Still it was minutes before he could make himself heard.

Eventually, the audience quietened and he began 'Mr Liddell, you have shown that none can pass you but the examiner.'

More applause silenced him for a while and then he went on to remind those present of how Olympic champions in the past were crowned with olive wreaths by the High Priest of Zeus. Amid more applause, he then 'crowned' Eric with an oleaster wreath. This is a plant of the olive family and the nearest to the original leaf that Sir Alfred Ewing had been able to obtain from the nearby Edinburgh Royal Botanical Gardens only days before.

After the crowning came the presentation of a Greek-inscribed scroll which, translated, read thus:

The University of Edinburgh congratulates
Eric Henry Liddell
Olympic victor in the 400 metres

Happy the man who the wreathed games essaying
Returns with laurelled brow
Thrice happy victor thou, such speed displaying
As none hath showed till now
We joy, and Alma Mater for thy merit
Proffers to thee this crown
Take it, Olympic Victor. While you wear it
May Heaven never frown.

Eric Liddell, the new BSc; Olympic champion and possibly the greatest athlete Scotland would ever know stood silently accepting it all with grace. But as the last words of the principal faded, that mischievous grin slowly spread itself across his face. He looked upon himself as a big joke and the crown was a means of giving the people much pleasure. He laughed with them.

Suddenly some of his friends leapt forward. Once again he was hoisted on their broad shoulders to be borne from the splendour of McEwans Hall, out into the street and carried all the way to St Giles Cathedral in the High Street for a graduation service.

Crowds lined the streets as he went. They waved, cheered and applauded. Shy and unassuming as Eric always was, he recognised that this was their great day. They had an Olympic champion of their own. Borne aloft in his hood and gown – Scottish graduates wear a hooded gown and not the cap or mortar-board of most countries – Eric waved and laughed from his human chariot.

At the steps of the cathedral he was permitted to alight and in that moment he remembered Guy Butler and the thousands who had not returned to their homes in triumph.

Somehow, the crowd sensed his thoughts and they were quiet. Eric looked about him and at his recently vacated chariot then he said for all to hear:

'In the dust of defeat as well as in the laurels of victory there is a glory to be found if one has done his best.'

After the religious service at the cathedral, there was a luncheon where again Eric was lauded.

Just as he believed all the ceremony of the day was finished, as he was leaving the cathedral yet another surprise was waiting for him. Students and graduates alike had gathered outside, all proudly dressed in their University blue. And with them was a carriage. Laughingly they invited Eric and Sir Alfred Ewing to take their seats. Then they themselves drew the carriage along. It travelled the Royal Mile on into Princes Street and arrived at the principal's home where tea was waiting.

What a day it had been for Edinburgh and for the Olympic victor! How lonely he had felt hours before with none of his family present! Now he looked back to see that the entire city had shared the day with him. They were all a part of one big family. He wasn't alone.

From then on, every day there were civic receptions; luncheons; teas; speeches, and always crowds; cheers and applause.

In China his family were overjoyed at his victory and even they were receiving cablegrams congratulating them on their son's triumph.

Just one week after his return from Paris, Eric was back in London to run for the British Empire against the United States of America. He was entered for the 4×440 yards relay and his 'leg' was run in under 46 seconds. Then it was back to Edinburgh and more receptions.

He was asked why did he think he was able to run at such speeds and laughingly he told them 'My ancestors came from the border counties between England and Scotland. And as they were constantly making raids into England they learned to run very fast in order to get back across the Scottish border as quickly as possible.'

His listeners appreciated his humour but they sensed the truth lay in his following words 'The fact is, I don't like to be beaten.'

It was at one of the luncheons a week later when Eric took everyone by complete surprise. As usual he was asked to make a speech. In it he gave special thanks to the man sitting beside him; Tom McKerchar, his trainer who had first seen him at Powderhall. It seemed a lifetime since, yet it was only three years. The crowd applauded Tom after Eric had finished his speech. Then, just as everyone expected him to sit down, he stood looking about him. His smile faded and everyone grew uneasy, wondering what had happened.

In his soft voice, with slow words he told them he had been offered a post at the College in Tientsin. From that day onwards, he wished to devote all his time to studying for the missionary work he had always planned to do in China.

An awed silence fell on the diners. They understood what he was saying. The Olympics were over! It was time for the rejoicing to stop.

In front of them stood, not the great athlete, but Eric Liddell the evangelist and he was asking – begging them to set him free; free to lay aside his olive wreath. In that moment he seemed a greater victor than ever before and his wishes were respected. He was still *their* champion but above all, he was *God's*.

Eric asked for a year's deferment of his teaching appointment in Tientsin. He needed time to go on more campaigns in Britain now he had graduated from the University. Also he had promised to visit Germany the following year where he would campaign amongst the British Army of Occupation on the Rhine. These were the troops left there from the Great War.

He applied for a place at the Congregational College in Edinburgh to study theology. This meant having to leave the Medical Missionary Hostel and the friendly Taylors to take up residence at the college. Nevertheless, they would always be his friends and he was welcome to visit any time.

Once in Tientsin, he would be teaching chemistry but he'd promised to take charge of sports as well, so he kept up his training and took part in many more athletic meetings.

At weekends he was travelling all over Scotland and England on the 'crusades'. On weekdays he was attending all the classes he could at the Congregational College. Evenings were spent either studying or training. Only a man of his physical and spiritual strength could sustain such a punishing programme.

Eric always found it hard to refuse anyone anything and he was asked to form committees; sit on committees; play football or run for charity.

Even with his 'olive wreath' laid aside, Eric Liddell's name attracted admiring crowds wherever he went. At times so many gathered they would be turned away. At religious meetings buildings would be crammed with people crushed shoulder to shoulder.

The numbers of people who turned to God during those crusades of 1924–25 were beyond all expectations. The evangelists spoke in theatres, churches, public houses, schools, dance-halls, social clubs; anywhere where an *audience* would collect together.

In that year, Eric gained so much knowledge of missionary work his confidence grew and grew until he was able to hide much of his shyness. His name was spoken in sermons as an example to the young. He was invited to Eltham where the students assembled in the quadrangle to greet the 'old boy'. Eric couldn't help remembering the day he caused the headmaster to almost fall off his bike. But on that day, the students embarrassed *him* when they cheered so loudly and for so long they could be heard a mile away.

In the 1920s, people were as likely to hero-worship sportsmen as they would film or pop stars in the years to come. And it was inevitable that Eric Liddell would attract fans in their thousands.

It was because of this that he came to meet someone who would become a lifelong friend and provide him with the home life he yearned for so much.

Elsa McKechnie was a 14-year-old pupil of the George Watson Ladies College in Edinburgh and every day she scoured the newspapers for news – no matter how unimportant – of her idol. Her family and friends teased her about it, but she didn't mind. Eric Liddell was someone to admire and she wasn't ashamed of her affection for him.

After school she would cycle to the Congregational College to stand outside in the hope of catching a glimpse of her hero. Sometimes she was lucky. Sometimes she returned home disappointed. There were many girls at her college who shared Elsa's admiration for Eric and this gave her an idea. Why not form an Eric Liddell Fan Club?

First, she asked her friends and they were all eager to join. Then, thinking it only polite to ask his permission, she wrote to Eric and asked if he would give a signed acceptance of such a club.

Of course, with his nature, rather than thinking he was honouring Elsa, he believed he was being honoured and wrote back, giving his full support but adding, 'I don't know what I'm letting myself in for.'

When the fan club was formed, it had very strict rules which read:

1. Each member is entitled to one page of this book, in which a poem or account of Eric Liddell must be

inserted, which must be approved by the committee.
2. Before becoming a member of this club the person in question must undergo an oral examination, put by the founder.
3. Each member must promise three things a) Always to uphold Eric Liddell. b) To attend all meetings arranged by the committee. c) To keep all rules of the club. It is also desirable that members should use the Eric Liddell lines.
4. Members will be presented with a photo of Eric Liddell and must promise to put it in a place of honour.
5. Should any member of this club do anything unworthy of the club, the committee will at once expel the member in question.

                                          BY ORDER

Eric had always loved children but his way of life kept him apart from them — even his own sister and brother. Now, with this little girl and her friends forming a fan club he felt as honoured as when receiving medals, cups or olive wreaths.

His fans were well behaved too. There was no shouting or screaming, simply a quiet respect for a wonderful man.

After the club was formed with Eric's approval, Elsa wrote to thank him and added at the bottom of her letter that she would be pleased if he would come to her home for tea. Not for one moment did she think he would accept her invitation. Her family and friends teased her for her nerve.

But not surprisingly, Eric was delighted and accepted immediately. The day he was due to go for tea, Elsa raced home from college on her bike to meet her idol and Eric proved to be everything she'd ever imagined and more. He seemed perfect and her parents thought so too. From then until he left for China, Eric was a frequent visitor to their home. He really appreciated sharing their happy family life. It was something that had been missing from his for so long.

It was understandable that people should think Eric perfect. His friend, DP, now the Reverend Dr David Patrick Thomson, said he was the most 'Godlike man' he ever knew. And Elsa showed her admiration when she planted orange nasturtiums and different coloured Virginia stock in her garden to come up displaying his initials; EHL. She may not have if his parents had not changed them round just before he was officially registered at birth.

Just as when he refused to run on a Sunday, Eric carried his Christian ideals with him wherever he went.

There was the time before a race when a black athlete was left kicking his heels on the grass verge beside the track while everyone about him chatted to each other. Eric was the one to go over and engage him in conversation.

On another occasion when the athletes were lined up for a 440 yards race, Eric realised he had the best position on the inside of the track. There was no staggering for a bend in those days and he knew the man drawn on the outside was a poor runner compared with himself and the rest. So, being Eric, he went over and asked the man if they could exchange places. 'I always feel happier on the outside,' he said.

When it was almost time for Eric to leave Scotland, every newspaper reported his imminent departure. Once again all his athletic glory was related together with accounts of what he aimed to do in China.

One newspaper carried a cartoon of Eric running in his white vest, black shorts, spiked boots – and a clergyman's 'dog collar'. Underneath, the caption read:

'For China now another race he runs
As sure and straight as those Olympic ones
And if the ending's not so simply known
We'll judge he'll make it, since his speed's his own'

Edinburgh was so proud of her Olympic champion there was grief in the city at losing him. There was pride too in the role he'd chosen for his future life.

It was quite a sad time for Eric too. He was returning to China where his much-loved family awaited him. Yet, most of his life had been spent in Scotland and although China was the land of his birth, it was his parents' Scottish blood that flowed through his veins. Many of his relatives lived there and all of his friends. As for the city itself, he dreaded leaving its splendid churches; its ancient history and buildings. He loved Princes Street and the Royal Mile that stretched from the castle on the hill to Holyrood House. He'd grown to love the University and even Powderhall. There were so many memories to take with him.

His last race in Scotland was at the Scottish AAA Championships. Knowing it was the last time they would see him run, 12,000 people came to watch and cheer him on to victory. Eric won all three of his races; the 100, 220 and 440 yards.

At last, on a balmy evening in July, 1925, the time came for him to leave. He came out of the college door where he knew the carriage was waiting to take him to Waverley Station. But what a sight met his eyes. The carriage was there – festooned in coloured ribbons and streamers. Instead of two horses, in the shafts were two teams of college students, University students, former students and friends. All in their various uniforms they drew the carriage along the busy thoroughfare; from Hope Terrace, along Clerk Street, Nicolson Street, over South Bridge and North Bridge and on to the station.

Crowds lined the streets, some laughing and waving – others unashamedly weeping. It seemed the great, bustling city had come to a standstill to say farewell to her favourite son.

And it seemed he would never really be permitted to lay down his crown.

At the station more cheering crowds were waiting to give him a memorable send-off. In these situations, Eric was able to cast off his shyness. It was almost as though he too was cheering Edinburgh's Olympic victor along with the crowd; as though he, Eric Liddell wasn't personally involved. He could enter into the joy and wave back cheerily.

But then, just as the train began to move slowly away from the platform, he grew sombre as memories flooded his mind.

Even the crowd sensed his feelings and as one, they began to sing one of his favourite hymns – but not the one where the lonely, lost lamb always made him cry as a child.

As the train gathered speed, Eric settled down to think of all that lay ahead of him.

He'd left China as a little boy of five. He was returning as a twenty-three-year-old man. The years between had seen many changes in China and one of them was the means of getting there. It was overland nearly all the way; a much quicker and maybe more exciting route which cut the old one by a third of the time.

On reaching London, instead of boarding a liner for the six-week voyage, Eric simply took a ferry across the English Channel. From there a train took him across Europe to Vladivostok in Russia where he boarded a train on the new

Trans-Siberian Railway. This cut right through the Ural Mountains and on into China. Conveniently, the Trans-Siberian Railway terminus was in Tientsin.

Actually, Eric didn't go direct to Tientsin. His family were on holiday at Pei-Tai Ho and he joined them there for a well earned rest.

At the end of his two week journey, Eric was overjoyed to see his family again. They were all waiting at Pei-Tai-Ho village station for him – all except Robbie. Since returning to China, Robbie had married and was working out at the hospital in Siao Chang. But he and his wife were coming to join the family the day after Eric arrived.

James and Mary were so happy to have the entire family reunited – and not merely for a brief spell as on so many occasions in the past.

It was a wonderful holiday lasting six weeks. There were picnics, swimming, sun-bathing and talk, talk, talk. This went on constantly as they all caught up on the time they'd been apart.

There was one grey cloud over that holiday though. Eric had looked forward to the church services where his father would often be preacher. Instead, James' friends asked if Eric would take the services as they were for missionaries from several countries. All Mission Societies owned holiday cottages at Pei-Tai-Ho.

This was a terrifying ordeal for such a shy young man. During his long evangelical campaigns, he'd learned how to handle audiences. He could cope with a vast sporting crowd too. But now, he was expected to preach to people who had spent their entire lives preaching Christianity to others – and he was not yet ordained.

The morning services were in Chinese; the evening services in English. Only then did Eric realise with a shock that he'd forgotten most of the Chinese he'd considered to be his 'mother tongue' when a child. There and then, while on holiday, he began to revise the language in readiness for starting at the college.

He was asked to take Sunday School classes for the missionaries' children as well but he didn't mind that at all.

Most of James and Mary's friends knew Eric from when they, themselves were in Britain on leave. Others had only known him as a small boy. The rest had just met him for the first time. To one family, the McKenzies from Canada, he was a complete stranger. But like the McKechnies in Edinburgh, they thought he was perfect. And so did their two young daughters, Florence and Margaret. They would have their parents helpless with laughter when they came home from Sunday School to tell them all about Mr Liddell's latest jokes and tricks.

The more staid missionaries disapproved of all the loud laughter and giggling coming from the Sunday School. But Eric loved to make children happy and, with his sense of fun, it wasn't difficult. He didn't see how joy and laughter could be sinful. They were two of God's greatest gifts.

At last, as with all holidays, the time at Pei-Tai-Ho was drawing to an end. James thought Eric should go on to Tientsin ahead of the others to get settled in before the college re-opened and he would go with him.

Just as when his parents first went to China, Eric had chosen a very bad time to come back.

Sun Yat Sen, the revolutionary who had helped China to become a republic, died suddenly in 1925. Although the communists already had a strong hold on the country, their powers began to grow; there were strikes everywhere and all sorts of minor rebellions.

On May 25th, weeks before Eric left Scotland, there had been the infamous 'Shanghai Incident'. Some Chinese workers had been dismissed from their work in a Japanese-owned factory. Other workers came out on strike in sympathy for them, then college students joined them to make a protest march through the city. British police fired on them and one of the marchers was killed.

This resulted in the whole city of Shanghai going on strike, a strike that spread to other cities including Tientsin. As a further protest against the 'Shanghai Incident' and the British in general, students threatened to boycott the Anglo-Chinese College and refused to attend when it re-opened in September after the summer holiday.

At a meeting in Pei-Tai-Ho, it was Eric who suggested the threat should be ignored. Let the college open as usual and see what happened. As he was newly appointed to the staff and also the youngest, he wondered later if he should have spoken out like that but everyone agreed it was the best thing to do.

Eric had felt it a real honour to be given a post at the college and there were some who felt it was because of his father being such a well respected man. It was nothing of the sort. Dr Lavington Hart, the college principal, was himself a BSc who had given up a promising career in science to devote his life to missionary work. In Eric Liddell he saw a kindred soul, and anyway, like the headmaster at Eltham, he too believed in rearing 'healthy minds in healthy bodies'. Sport was the best way to prove that theory and who better than Eric to supervise.

The Anglo-Chinese College was an impressive building of grey brick walls and towers. Called by the Chinese 'The Hall of New Learning' it had opened shortly after Eric was born in 1902. At first it had only five pupils under twelve years of age, but when it became a boarding as well as day school, the numbers increased rapidly.

It was the first school in China to provide for the sons of

wealthy parents. Until then, missionaries tended to educate only the peasant class. But Dr Hart saw things differently. It was politicians, doctors, bankers and other such people who held all the power and influence in the land. To draw their children into the Christian fold would be far more effective than those who had no power. Already there was a lot of work being done for the financially poor. The wealthy were impoverished in another way if they didn't know the Christian God.

Dr Hart had been proud when the first students arrived, carrying their own bed-rolls, rice-bowls and chopsticks. They wouldn't surrender to western customs easily, he thought. But the fact they were there at all was enough to satisfy the good doctor.

9: Life's Mission

Called locally, 'The City of the Heavenly Ford', the name given to it by the westerners seemed more appropriate, 'The Manchester of the North'. Naturally, although Eric was born in Tientsin, he had no memories of it, but his parents had.

When James and Mary returned there to take up yet another mission post, they noticed a lot of changes. But compared with their village home in Siao Chang and their more recent home in the lovely capital, Peking, Tientsin was still mainly a big, rambling, dirty, industrial trading port.

The River Haiho was still always flooding its banks. There were the usual gales and dust storms in the dry summer, and winter temperatures were always below zero.

It was still a divided city with its narrow, smelly alleyways of hovels and its Devil's Market where thieves, opium dealers and forgers traded their wares.

Yet, there had been a lot of improvement in the years since they'd lived there before.

After the Boxer rebellion, the city walls were dismantled. Where they used to stand were tarmacadam roads with electric trams. Three main railway lines came into the city – one being the Trans-Siberian terminus.

The city had gained three universities – yet there was illiteracy everywhere among the poor.

And now, stretching out from the city centre, in sharp

contrast to the slum area near the docks, were suburbs with beautiful homes. Here lived politicians, teachers, doctors, and wealthy merchants. Thirty countries had concessions there as well.

Standing on the River Haiho, though thirty miles from the sea, Tientsin was the main port for Peking with mile upon mile of wharves.

To spread the world news there were *seven* daily newspapers. The streets of decorative arches teemed with cyclists, pedestrians, trams, rickshaws and expensive foreign cars.

James and Mary did most of their work in the cluster of hovels on the poor side of the city but their mission home was in the area where the foreign concessions stood. The address Eric had always sent his mail to was No 2 London Mission, Tientsin, North China. Now, with their family complete again the Liddells were to move into No 6 which was more roomy.

It was a four-storey building of large rooms. James' study and the dining-room were on the ground floor slightly apart from the kitchens. All the living rooms were on the second floor with bedrooms and bathrooms on the third. But of all places, Eric asked if he could have his bedroom in the attic next to the lumber-room.

There he could be alone yet know he had the comfort of his family close at hand. He could have peace and also be in a position to survey everything way below him, especially the tennis courts where many boisterous games would no doubt be played now he was home.

His parents were middle-aged now but they still worked as hard as ever. James worked between a church in the city and several in outlying districts. This sometimes kept him away from home for days at a time.

Mary went visiting poor homes with other mission

women. Jenny was a kindergarten teacher and Ernest was at school. All the same they managed to spend a lot of time together and the house was often full of visitors, sometimes just for meals, sometimes to spend a few days.

At this time, Eric was beginning to have fears about the teaching appointment he'd been given. It wouldn't be at all like the Sunday School classes at Pei-Tai-Ho. His students would be Chinese for one thing. For another, he would really be *teaching*. Giving instructions, perhaps sometimes orders, wouldn't come easy to Eric with his easy-going nature, even though he would be dealing in his favourite subjects; religion, science and sport.

Most of the students went on to university. Others followed their fathers' trade or profession and former students were to be found all over the world in positions of high authority and responsibility. It was frightening to think that these boys would be Eric's responsibility for several years.

There were five British teachers and twenty-five Chinese teachers there and, Eric was pleased to learn, his lessons would all be conducted in English. His Chinese was still very poor.

Therefore, at a meeting just before the new term started, he was shocked to hear that he was expected to teach English. It had always been his worst subject throughout his school life.

When he got home and told his family, Jenny teasingly tried to comfort him with the fact — as the students were Chinese their English grammar was sure to be worse than his. Eric took her teasing well but he was filled with self-doubt.

On his first day there, when it re-opened in September, despite the threat of a boycott, 150 of the 400 students turned up. The following week, 300 attended. It had clearly been wise to open.

All the boys came from wealthy families, and while some walked to school, others were chauffeur-driven in Rolls Royces and Cadillacs. But every one of them wore the simple, floor-length Chinese gown of deep-blue cotton.

Nearly all were from non-Christian homes so half an hour each morning was reserved for their devotions. This didn't simply mean saying or singing set prayers and hymns. They weren't enough. It was a time when they were introduced to and encouraged to lead a more humane way of life.

There was far more to being a Christian than merely believing in Jesus Christ. The essential part was to believe in what he stood for; kindness, love, generosity and gentleness; qualities which were rather alien to the heathen Chinese but which came naturally to Eric Liddell and to the college principal. What better disciple could the Lord have chosen to teach these qualities than Eric?

Once the news leaked out that their teacher had achieved great fame and success in his own land, the students were surprised. Why should he give it all up to come to China to tell them of Christ? They decided this Christian God must be truly wonderful.

The college masters were encouraged to take a personal interest in their students' lives, both inside and outside the college. For the four years they were there, rather than move up from class to class, teacher to teacher, they stayed together throughout their education.

Eric's boys were fortunate in having a 'house father' like him. So much of his free time was given over to them and their problems. They even went to his house and in the privacy of his study up in the attic, they were able to discuss anything that was troubling them. And no matter how they doubted and questioned the existence of Jesus Christ, Eric never lost his patience. His faith was too strong to take offence.

It wasn't long before many of the boys were asking to be baptised into the Christian church. Oddly enough their non-Christian parents encouraged this. They could see the effect Christian teaching was having on their sons and realised it was for the good.

There was one subject Eric was always reluctant to discuss though. Never one to boast, he got embarrassed when they wanted to hear all about his sporting record. At the same time, when anyone asked to see his trophies, he hadn't the heart to refuse them.

Whenever he went for his medals it meant hunting in drawers and sorting them out, every time. To overcome this problem, he made a set of wooden boxes with slide out trays in which all the medals were set out in order. From then on, all he had to do was hand over the boxes to would-be viewers to help themselves. And with each medal labelled, it not only saved time, it protected Eric from having to say '*I* won this for . . .' or '*I* got this for . . .'

Getting the students interested in sport for themselves was more difficult than introducing them to Christianity or even teaching English.

Well, not sport in general but football and running. They already liked boxing, wrestling and fencing. In winter they enjoyed skating.

But football was hated with the students complaining that the weather was either too hot or, at 30 degrees below zero, too cold. In a way, Eric sympathised with them. There was no proper pitch and no running track to speak of. The ground was hard and rough with every game or race resulting in bad grazes, scratches and cuts.

In all the twenty-three years since the college opened, the students had insisted on wearing their long, blue cotton gowns for sport. When Eric first appeared in his vest and shorts they thought he looked indecent. Actually, although at that time, shorts were rather long, Eric's always seemed that bit longer and came down to his knees.

As for Eric, he thought they looked as ridiculous as the athletes training in their overcoats at Powderhall. As they ran about, they tripped over their own and each other's gowns but he didn't dare let them see the smile that threatened to give his thoughts away.

The Chinese idea of sport was to take part only when they were sure they would win, not to play at all if it was raining, attack the referee if they disagreed with him and think nothing of taking the entire team off the field if one got hurt – no matter how slight the injury.

Eventually, they did see the sense in wearing shorts. It was Eric's speed that did this. In a long gown he could never have run so fast – and probably not at all for laughing.

Unfortunately, when they wore shorts, the injuries from falls or tackles were more severe.

There was only one solution. They must have proper sports facilities. The whole of Tientsin was without a stadium of any kind so Eric set about getting one built. A vast area of wasteland was reclaimed and with Eric supervising, the stadium became one of the best in Asia as it was designed on the one at Stamford Bridge, England.

It opened in time for the Annual International Athletic Games and, for the first time, the Chinese public saw Eric in action. No one could believe that a man could achieve such speeds and this strengthened their belief in his God.

At this time, Robbie and his wife, with their baby daughter, were working at Siao Chang. But it was so long since he'd seen his brother run, he was determined to be present at Eric's next race.

He bought a second-hand motor-bike and persuaded Annie Buchan, the hospital matron, to go with him to Tientsin to see Eric. She'd never met him but was a great

113

fan. Annie was terrified as they bumped and wobbled over the sun-baked land.

At Tientsin, they saw more than they'd expected to. As the runners set off, a press photographer ran on the track to get a photograph of Eric at full speed. The poor man didn't know just what 'Eric's full speed' was, and the crowd held its breath as the athlete drew ever closer. Of course, Eric, as usual, had his head back on his shoulders, seeing nothing but a bright, blue sky. On he came, pelting down the track, flattening the photographer with camera and tripod flying high in the air. Eric sprawled on his face, unconscious and his doctor brother and Annie ran to his assistance. They reached him just as he was coming round. He looked up with a big grin and said 'I was only winded.'

During the following years, Eric kept running – and winning, yet strangely, he wasn't asked to join the British team for the 1928 Olympic Games in Amsterdam, Holland. Later, he discovered this was because no one outside of China knew he was still running. The winners of the 200 and 400 metre races at Amsterdam were the French and Japanese. And in the very week they won, Eric ran the same races in Tientsin in *faster* times.

Once the authorities heard of this, they wrote and asked if he would run for the British team in the 1932 Olympics at Los Angeles, in the USA. Eric replied that he would then be thirty years of age and much too old to compete.

His races in China made him known to people outside the missionary and college community and they always wanted to hear all about his past successes. To hide his blushes, Eric would always choose some funny incident to relate. There was that disastrous American trip of 1923 when he lost his races, his luggage and all the gifts and souvenirs he'd brought back. There was the time he fell off the back of his friend's motor-bike.

There was another hilarious story he loved to tell. He'd been to an athletic meeting at Darien, sited on a small peninsula across the river from Tientsin, and his last ferry back was at three o'clock in the afternoon. The meeting wouldn't be over at that time. But as Eric was entered for an early race, the 200 yards, even if he reached the final he would have ample time to get to the boat.

At the meeting, someone asked him to enter the 400 yards as well and he did. Modest as ever, he didn't expect to reach the final but, when he did, he found to his horror it would be run at 2.30, a mere half-hour before his boat left. He immediately booked a taxi and asked if the driver could be waiting at the sportsground entrance when the race ended. As soon as he heard the off for the 400 yard race, he was to start the car and Eric would keep on going, from the tape, out of the ground and jump into the taxi.

Of course, Eric won the race and felt a bit of a fool as the crowd of 50,000 cheered and he kept on running towards the main exit in his vest, shorts and spiked boots. But there was something he'd overlooked. The band began to play the winner's national anthem. As he heard them strike up God Save The King (George V was on the throne at that time) the crowd stood in respectful silence and Eric managed to come to a standstill. The band seemed to be playing so slowly and his heart was thumping from running and panic at missing his boat. As the last note faded, he sprang into motion again, still heading for the gate and his taxi. Off went the band again, playing La Marseillaise in honour of the Frenchman who'd come second. Eric 'threw out his anchor' as he said later and again he came to a halt.

By the time they finished playing, he had just fifteen minutes to reach the docks. He left the ground, leapt into the taxi and the driver accelerated as though driving a 'getaway car'. They ran into all sorts of traffic hold-ups and got to the dockside to see the boat slowly moving away from the quay. Eric stared in disbelief and was about to turn and walk away when suddenly, as the boat reached the narrowed harbour walls, a gust of wind blew the little ferry a bit back to port. Eric sprinted down the quay with his luggage and just before the boat recovered its balance, he took off, cleared an unbelievable fifteen feet stretch of water and landed on his back on the deck in front of startled passengers.

Later he denied it was fifteen feet, claiming it was much less, but then he would. Everyone who saw the feat agreed on the distance and from then on he was known as The Flying Scotsman.

In 1929, after a long term in China, James and Mary were due for leave but, before they went, all the family took a holiday in Pei-Tei-Ho.

Eric organised hikes, picnics and rambles for the children there, and they got up to all kinds of tricks. Some of the stuffy parents chastised their children when they returned and told them what they'd got up to while they were out.

'You should be ashamed to behave that way when you're with Mr Liddell,' they often said, not knowing it was Mr Liddell's idea in the first place.

Eric often arranged sing-songs on the beach at night and one of the favourite songs was 'Underneath the Spreading Chestnut Tree' – a very popular song at that time. He always started to mime to the words and everyone would follow him. But after the first couple of lines, mischief always got the better of him. He would do all the right mimes in the wrong places until no one knew where they were up to. It always ended in everyone rolling about in the sand in hysterics.

At the end of the holiday, Eric's parents left Tientsin for Britain together with Jenny and Ernest. They remembered how they had left their two small sons in Britain while they returned to China. Now it was Eric and Robbie who stood waving them goodbye.

Eric was due for leave the following year and his parents would still be in Scotland because they had earned a two-year absence from work.

No 6, London Mission had been given over to another family and this added to Eric's sadness at losing his family. They'd spent four wonderfully happy years there and now he was to take up residence in a flat at the college.

The flat was shared with three others but it was quite big with a dining-room, sitting-room, four bedrooms and studies. They had a servant, Kwei-Lin, who did all the shopping, cooking and cleaning for them. He provided breakfast at 7.30; Chinese lunch at noon; a typically English afternoon-tea and an English dinner at night.

They all got on very well together although they all had different personalities. Eric was more religious than the others but they respected this and never interrupted him during his morning meditations. He still began his day with a quiet time when he spoke to God, his closest friend, and planned his day.

His colleagues loved to play billiards and introduced Eric to the game. He soon became as good at that as he was at running. Another flat-mate collected Chinese stamps and Eric became interested in that too.

Now his family were gone and Robbie was away in Siao Chang he had more spare time to pursue different interests. There were no longer the cosy, family evenings to take up the time. He missed the family dreadfully, especially his mother whom he adored. It was always his hope that, someday, he would have a wife just like her. He didn't realise then that the girl was close at hand.

Knowing how Eric must miss his own people, the

McKenzies encouraged him to spend a lot of time with them. They lived the same cosy, happy, home life as the Liddells and the house was often teeming with visitors.

Florence had grown into a very beautiful girl. She was rather small, had dark, curly hair and dark flashing eyes. Just like Eric, she was full of life and loved fun. They were always playing practical jokes on each other and, for revenge, Eric called her 'Flossie' – a name she hated.

When it came time for the summer holidays at Pei-Tai-Ho, Eric went off to share a cottage with his three flat-mates and the McKenzies moved in a few doors away.

It was the usual holiday of tennis, concerts, picnics and hikes.

Flo had been in love with Eric for a long time but no one suspected it – not even Eric. But it was during this holiday that people began to suspect *he* was in love with *her*. At that time, he was twenty-eight and Florence was eighteen. He knew some of the 'stuffy' people would disapprove if he asked her to go out alone with him for walks so, poking fun at them, he would suggest as many as a dozen friends should all go for a walk or go to the local tea-room. On these occasions, Flo always felt herself lucky to be included. She didn't realise it was an excuse to be with her. No one thought it except the three friends he lived with, and they teased him about Flo all through the holiday.

One day, someone suggested going on a walking tour to Mount Pei-Niu-Ting which overlooked the seaside resort. A hermit had lived there for many years and everyone was curious about him.

There were ten in the party: Eric, Robbie, Flo and her sister Margaret and six other missionaries. It would be a four-day trip and they needed a lot of supplies. They had ten donkeys but as one carried the food, tents and bedding rolls not everyone could ride all the time. It was a long, hard climb over the rough track of a dried-up river bed. It was rock-strewn and whoever was walking at any time had a painful trek with stones digging into their shoe soles. After the river bed came a steep, narrow mountain track overlooking a great yawning valley where a carpet of boulders awaited anyone unfortunate enough to slip.

Everyone took care of their companions but it was noticeable how much extra care Eric took of Flo.

At the end of one particularly difficult stretch on the mountain pass, they all stopped for a much appreciated meal then settled down for a well earned nap. Suddenly, one of the older missionaries sat up with a startled look. 'Where's Eric?' he asked anxiously.

They all shot up, fearing he'd slipped and fallen. Then Margaret McKenzie laughed and pointed way ahead to the summit of the track. 'Look!'

There, at the highest point stood a lone figure, gazing out into infinity then glancing down at the world below him. The wife of the man who first noticed he was missing said, 'That will be Eric's idea of taking a rest.'

Of course, it wouldn't have been much effort for Eric to make that climb but he could simply have lain down for a sleep in the hot midday sun. Instead he would choose to reach a height that would take him as near to God and the heavens as possible to spend a few moments in meditation and prayer.

Maybe it was in those moments that he decided Florence was the girl he had waited for for so many years. She had been in his Sunday School class when she was a little girl, and in recent years she had played the organ at the Sunday School in Tientsin where Eric had just been made Superintendent.

Like Eric's mother – Mary Reddin as she was when James Liddell first met her – Flo and Margaret McKenzie planned to become nurses. They were due to leave China to take up their training in Toronto, Canada – their parents' homeland – shortly before Eric was due to go on leave to Britain.

After the Pei-Tai-Ho holiday, when they were all back in Tientsin, Eric proposed marriage to Flo and she accepted. Again, like his parents, it would be a long time before they married because of Flo's training. But both the McKenzie and Liddell families were overjoyed when they heard the news.

In Eric's letter home to tell his family, he asked his mother and Jenny if they would buy for him an engagement ring with five diamonds exactly like the one his father had given his mother. They bought it from the same jewellers and sent it out to China where it arrived just in time for Eric and Flo to get engaged before she left for Canada.

Within a matter of weeks after that, Eric too was on his way back to Britain for a long leave.

10: Heartaches and Happiness

Actually, Eric had planned to cross the Pacific to Canada to spend some time with Flo and her family who had just gone home on leave. Having him there gave the McKenzies the opportunity to introduce their future son-in-law to all their relatives and friends in Toronto.

The young man with his vivid, laughing blue eyes and dazzling smile was taken to everyone's heart. Pure goodness shone out of him and any place he went seemed to light up in his presence yet he was so shy.

After a short stay in Canada he was off again, this time across the Atlantic to his family in Scotland. This journey was entirely different from either of the other two he'd made; first as a child sailing from Shanghai port then as a young man when he returned via the Trans-Siberian Railway.

He intended studying for two terms at the Edinburgh Congregational College where he'd studied before. This time he intended returning to China as an ordained minister of the church.

His parents and the rest of the family would have a lot of his time and so would his friends. DP Thomson had invited him to spend time at his home and the McKechnies had invited him to their home. He was really looking forward to the next twelve months.

Since leaving Edinburgh, little Elsa McKechnie had not only sent him letters, birthday and Christmas cards. She

sent valentine cards and poems she'd written about him.
There were those who thought she had a 'schoolgirl crush'
on Eric but they were wrong. It was simply 'hero worship'
and respect for a great man.

There was one thing about Eric's leave that he'd never
even considered. The newspapers were full of articles about
Scotland's famous athlete and his return home to
Edinburgh. Eric had taken it for granted that everyone
would have forgotten about him by then – he even hoped
they had.

But, without his knowledge, all sorts of events had been
arranged. There were so many, a special committee was set
up to deal with them.

One group was preparing to welcome the returning
Olympic Gold Medal winner. Another group was waiting
to greet the returning evangelist. Yet another thought of
him as a missionary to China coming home on leave.

He was booked to speak every Sunday morning,
afternoon and evening in England, Ireland and Scotland.
There wasn't a town in Scotland where he wasn't expected
to visit, from the southern border to the most northern tip
of the land.

He was also expected to open numerous sports meetings;
give lectures; attend reunion luncheons and dinners at his
former colleges and the University. At the first meeting he
attended, his *three* hosts represented: Scottish Football, The
Scottish Student Campaign Movement and The Scottish
Churches.

On top of all this, everywhere he went, everyone wanted
to know all about China. This amused Eric because the
Chinese always asked questions about Scotland.

Whenever he gave a talk on his work in China, he always
referred to a letter he received from one of his students of
English at the Tientsin College. It arrived shortly after

Eric reached Scotland and, though in no way was he making fun of the writer, he said it proved what a poor teacher he was. He had spent an afternoon trying to explain the meaning of sincerity, saying 'It comes from the Latin phrase *sine ceres* meaning "without wax".' He had told them that an examiner of sculpture always writes *sine ceres* on the bottom of a perfect piece of work, indicating that it has no flaws, therefore no cracks are filled in with wax.

At the bottom of the letter, his student had written: To Sir. Yours without wax.

There were two emotional upheavals in Eric's life during that first leave: one of joy, one of sadness. Since leaving China, Jenny had met and fallen in love with a young doctor. They were engaged and planned to marry while Eric was home. Robbie was due on leave too so the whole family would be present at the wedding. It was a grand affair and both Eric and Robbie were happy for their sister although it meant she wouldn't be returning to China with the rest of the family.

The sadness was when he learned that *none* of the family would be returning — except Robbie. His father's health hadn't been too good and the London Mission Society had decided to retire him from his arduous work.

Eric couldn't think of him being in poor health or of growing old. He was a strong, big-hearted Abraham Lincoln figure. In his son's eyes he would never change.

It seemed unfair that a family so fond of each other, should forever be parting. Always some of them were on the opposite side of the globe from the others. Still, Eric never questioned God's reason for this. He simply accepted that there must be one. A few years later he knew why the Lord had felt it better to keep them from returning to China.

Eric studied hard for his ordination and on the 22nd June, 1932, just before his leave ended, he became the

Reverend Eric Henry Liddell. It was a wonderful day for the Liddell family and especially for Eric. The Scottish Congregational Church, unknown to him, had arranged that his friend, DP – the Reverend Dr David Thomson – should officiate at the service.

He was due to leave Scotland in July to return to Toronto 'for health reasons' as someone jokingly said. He was *lovesick*.

Only days before he left he was at a friend's home to say his farewell when the friend asked if he would sign the 'visitors' book'. Eric laughed and duly signed his new title adding some Chinese after his name. His friend was curious and Eric explained it meant 'Keep smiling'. This was a phrase he often used and his friend said he knew someone else who said it a lot. He would show it to her.

He went on to tell Eric of this lady, Bella. Five years before she had been in a dreadful accident in which she was scalped, lost one eye and had the other eye badly damaged. Since then she'd suffered tortuous skin grafts, constantly had terrible headaches and was almost deaf and blind. Each month she returned to hospital to have the lashes pulled out of her remaining eye because they were growing inwards and were very painful. 'Yet,' the friend went on 'she goes through life being quite cheerful, telling everyone to "keep smiling". She'll be pleased to know it's your motto too. She's a great admirer of yours.'

Eric had winced at this catalogue of suffering and asked if Bella would mind if he visited her.

She was overjoyed at the prospect and throughout the hour he spent with her, she held his hand and told him she too worked for God. Her sufferings were *nothing* compared with some. But for those who complained over little things, she was able to show them how fortunate they really were.

The following morning, just as he was rushing out to

catch the London train to attend a final meeting there, a letter arrived for Eric. He pushed it in his pocket and read it on the journey. It was from Bella saying how happy his visit had made her. He read it again, then put it back in his pocket.

There was one other occupant in the railway carriage – a young man who was the picture of misery. Eric could always sense people's troubles. It was as though he could see through to their very soul. But anyone less sensitive could have seen that this young man had problems. He sat, head in hands and never once looked up.

Eric spoke to him, trying to cheer him up and, as so often happened to him, within minutes, the man was blurting out his life story.

He was a failure; poor at school; couldn't keep a job; didn't get on with his parents; couldn't keep a friend or girl friend. There was nothing to live for and he was going to kill himself.

Eric would never criticise anyone, even a suicide or a sinner. He preferred to befriend them and pray they would reform themselves. No matter what anyone did, he never ever accused them of being or doing wrong. Now he sat gazing at the bowed figure, wondering what on earth he could do or say to help. Then he remembered Bella. He drew the letter from his pocket and invited the young man to read it. He shrugged it off saying he couldn't be bothered.

'Just read it – once, please,' Eric begged in his soft, persuasive voice.

The man sullenly took it and read it. He read it again and shook his head in disbelief.

'And would you believe it? That lady takes care of four people,' Eric told him.

The man immediately felt ashamed of himself and, as if

by magic, he brightened up. Until then, he'd lost faith in God and himself. With a single sheet of paper from a good woman it was all restored in minutes. At London he left the train a different person from the one who'd boarded it at Edinburgh.

Eric wrote to Bella at once telling her what *she* had done and he quoted that letter many times in his life whenever he met anyone in similar circumstances. But it was always due to Bella – as if he played no part in it at all.

He spent all his time with his parents in the last days before he left to rejoin his other great love in Canada.

He would stay in Toronto for the last six weeks of his leave before going back to China. Flo was proud to greet her fiancé, the Rev Eric Liddell.

While he was there, the British Olympic team arrived to do some final training before carrying on to Los Angeles in America for the 1932 Games. When the authorities realised Eric Liddell was in town they invited him to go and meet them and perhaps give a talk on his past career.

If Eric had any regrets at not being one of the team he didn't show it. He gave them his best wishes and passed on a lot of advice to those athletes who'd never experienced an Olympics before.

When he and Flo parted, they knew it would be a year and a half before they met again, when her training was over.

By September, 1932, Eric was back in Tientsin for the new college term. Now, as an ordained minister he was expected to travel more, taking church services and doing general missionary work. He was still Sunday School Superintendent but now he was made college secretary and chairman of the sports committee.

This helped the time to pass more quickly before Florence returned to China to become Mrs Eric Liddell.

Robbie returned to China but he went straight out to the hospital at Siao Chang and the brothers didn't meet very often.

Eric was somehow really troubled at leaving the rest of the family behind. Then, one Sunday morning when he was taking a church service, he had just uttered one of his favourite Bible quotations, 'Lo, I am with you always', when he had the strangest experience. It was as if his father was standing beside him. The next morning, at breakfast, a cablegram arrived saying James had died suddenly.

Eric was overcome with grief. If only the Lord had taken him while he was in Scotland on leave, he could have been with him to the end. He would be there now to comfort his mother too, he thought. There must be a reason for it, he decided, and looking at the situation again he knew the answer. He might never have returned to China. Comforted by this thought, he thanked God for letting him spend so many hours with his father just before he left Edinburgh.

All the same, for himself, he felt like the lost lamb in the Sankey hymn. His father had influenced his life so much and now he was gone. Eric knew Robbie would be heart-broken too but he had his wife and little daughter for solace. As for his mother, she would be devastated at her loss and even with Jenny and Ernest close at hand, she would be surrounded by their sorrow as well as their comfort.

The only consolation Eric could find was in hard work and long letters home to Edinburgh and to Flo in Toronto. There were no speedy flights home in those days so he couldn't even attend his father's funeral.

As soon as the news got out, people came in dozens to tell Eric what his father had meant to them and to say it was James who had baptised them into the Christian church. Wherever he went, people spoke of the love, tenderness and years of hard work and self-sacrifice his father had put in during his years in China. All this made Eric very proud but it didn't ease his heartache much.

A week after Eric heard of his father's death he received the last letter James ever wrote to him. Ironically, it was written on November 27th, 1933, the day Flo was to sit her final exams. It told Eric how well James was feeling and to wish him well in his future work and in his marriage to Flo.

Now Eric realised why the Lord had let James live until Eric was back in China. He wasn't needed to give comfort and care for his ageing mother. Jenny and Ernest would do that. Eric's work was to continue where his father's had finished.

After Flo's exams, she and her mother were going to Britain to visit the Liddells in Edinburgh before returning to China. Mr McKenzie was travelling back ahead of them. Elsa McKechnie had arranged to take Flo and her mother sightseeing and to entertain them generally. And as James had just died, Mary was in need of a visit from her old friend.

By this time, Eric's three flatmates had all gone their separate ways and, apart from Kwei-Lin, the servant, Eric lived alone. This wasn't a bad thing because it meant he didn't have to find somewhere else to live after he was married. The flat would do nicely.

The next weeks were taken up in cleaning, painting and furnishing the place, making it fit for his bride. Missionaries tended not to own much furniture as they were always on the move so a bed or dining-suite or a three-piece suite could pass through many families during the course of its life. Jenny had owned her bedroom suite but she'd left it in China expecting to return there so Eric got that. He got chairs and a sofa from a family who were moving out to Shanghai and another bedroom suite from people going home on leave. At last, the flat was finished and Flo was due back.

She'd promised to send a telegram from Kale in Japan where their ship would put in before going on to Taku in China. Eric and her father, Hugh McKenzie, planned to surprise Flo and her mother by being there when they landed. However, they were disappointed when a letter came saying the ship had been delayed.

Together they'd taken the hour-long train journey to Taku only to have to put up for the night at a friend's house. Eric was on pins. It seemed years since he'd last seen Flo, yet it was only eighteen months. Because of it being winter, after Flo and her mother returned to Canada after their Edinburgh visit, they arranged to take the longer voyage to China to avoid bad conditions at sea. This route took them through the Polynesian islands of Hawaii and Honolulu which meant they wouldn't arrive until March; then there was the delay at Kale.

Early the next morning, Eric and Hugh McKenzie set off eagerly to greet the boat. Then they heard of another delay. The boat needed a 15-feet water clearance to enter the mouth of the river. But because of a fierce gale blowing, she didn't dare approach the harbour walls and this would mean missing the tide. If the winds dropped, there would be a mere 6-feet water clearance until later that evening.

Hugh and Eric returned to their friend's house where Eric paced up and down like a caged animal. Then the phone rang. The boat was risking coming in on a 13-feet clearance. It was a risky operation but she was getting battered in the gale and needed refuge.

Eric and Hugh McKenzie fell over each other in their haste to get down to the docks. They could see the lights glowing aboard the magnificent liner, *Empress of Canada*, and they both prayed for her safe berth, knowing the water could start to ebb at any moment. At her first attempt to dock, the *Empress* swung out, threatening to smash her stern against the quayside. Onlookers gasped and some turned away, afraid to watch the second try. But it was successful and everyone thanked God to see the great ship safely moored.

The two couples were so happy to be together again. Eric and Florence sat up all night, talking about her exams; Eric's work; James' death; their future home and the wedding plans. At half past five the following morning they were all on the train heading back for Tientsin.

Flo was really pleased at the way Eric had prepared the flat. Her one problem lay in unpacking all the trophies he'd kept hidden away for many years. Then she had to find places to display them all but she was so proud of her future husband, she was determined they would never be hidden again.

The wedding was three weeks later, on Tuesday, March 27th, in the Union Church where Eric was Superintendent and where Flo was once organist. It didn't have the grandeur of Shanghai's Cathedral but the church was crowded and the wedding itself was far more splendid than that of James and Mary Reddin in 1899. Miss Florence McKenzie had all her family around her. The Reverend Eric Henry Liddell had his brother, Robbie and his family present. And many friends of both bride and groom were there.

Given away by her father, Florence wore the white, satin dress her mother was married in. She carried a bouquet of pink carnations and, to Eric's surprise, she wore the lace veil Jenny wore for her wedding. Jenny gave it to Flo while she was staying in Scotland. With her shining eyes, her brilliant smile and gleaming, black, curly hair, Eric thought she had never looked more lovely.

Flo's friend, Gwyneth Rees, was bridesmaid. She wore a

long green silk gown with matching picture-hat and carried a posy of pink carnations.

Mrs McKenzie was in a flowing, black, georgette and lace gown with a pink carnation corsage.

The reception was at the McKenzie home in Cambridge Road, Teintsin, and, to receive their guests, the newly-weds stood under a huge silver bell decorated with more pink carnations. There were so many well-wishers, greetings cards, telegrams and presents. They seemed to come from all over the world, all conveying hopes for their future happiness – something which was to last such a short time. But on that spring day in China, like the flowers surrounding them, the years ahead seemed just a pink-scented promise.

After the reception, Eric and Flo went for a short honey-moon to Peiping, a few miles west of Tientsin.

Life in China was never peaceful for very long and even as they returned to Tientsin, more changes were in the wind. The communists were becoming more and more powerful throughout the land. At the same time, in the more northerly regions, an invader, Japan, was sending in troops who were meeting with little or no resistance – except from the great War Lords of China. These were wealthy, ruthless men with private armies. And they were feared as much by their own people as were the communists and Japanese invaders the War Lords were supposed to be defending them from.

Living in such political turmoil, Christianity appeared to represent sanity and was growing in popularity. Many college staff now held Bible classes for juniors when before, it was only Eric and one or two others who held them for the older boys. Yet, as this was going on, the government was ordering students to do military training. Eric was strongly opposed to this but he had to admit that some of them were fitter, better disciplined and smarter because of it.

Eric loved being a married man with a home of his own and within a year of marrying, he and Flo were the delighted parents of a little girl, Patricia. She was a noisy baby who howled through the night but they adored her. Eric took his turn pacing the floor with her while Flo got some sleep and when he felt tired the next morning, he never complained at having to take his class.

It was 1934 and Eric began writing a guide book for Sunday School teachers. This plus his teaching and church work took up a lot of time but every spare moment was spent with his family. A year later and another daughter arrived to add to their happiness. She introduced a bit of conflict into the home though.

Her parents simply couldn't decide upon a name they *both* liked. To be fair, Eric suggested the name should be picked 'out of a hat' so he wrote the name he liked – Heather – on a piece of paper and the name Flo liked was written on another. Both papers were tightly folded and placed in a hat for Flo to pick out. It was Eric's choice, Heather. Her mother was a bit disappointed but she accepted it had been done fairly. Then Eric, who had kept a perfectly straight face, burst out laughing and confessed he'd written Heather on both papers. His wife laughed so much at this she said they would keep the name to remind her not to trust him in future.

Now their happiness seemed complete and Eric was determined that his children would never be parted from their parents as he and Robbie had been. He even set about making little seats to strap on to the handlebars of his and Florence's bikes, so that the babies could go everywhere with them.

But alas, all his plans were soon to be turned upside down.

11: Danger Everywhere

In the June following Heather's birth, Flo went out to Pei-Tai-Ho to get the babies away from the grime and heat of summer in the city. As was usual for the husbands, Eric intended to join them there in the August. But before his holiday came around he received a terrible shock. The London Mission Society were being criticised for keeping too many missionaries at the Tientsin College when more 'field-workers' were wanted out on the Great Plain. Because Eric had once lived there and his brother was working in the hospital, he was asked if he would go to work in Siao Chang.

For many reasons he didn't want to go. He preferred being a college teacher to a village pastor and, he admitted to himself, modern city life was more comfortable than a hard existence on the Plain. Furthermore, his Chinese was nearly all *kwan-hwa* – the high language, and he would need to re-learn the basic *wan-hwa* he'd spoken as a child. But worst of all, it would mean leaving Florence and the children in Tientsin. Life in Siao Chang had become dangerous with all the political troubles that were going on.

He'd heard from Robbie all about the conditions there. It was no longer a peaceful little village with singing peasants working in the fields. There was drought and the crops were ruined from troops marching through constantly. The little hospital of 100 beds was overcrowded and the staff overworked. Babies were starving because their mothers were either dead or had no milk to feed them. They were surviving on the local bean curd milk made from soya with added sugar and calcium. This was good for them but only as an addition to their mothers' milk.

The farmers were disillusioned and had lost faith in the National government and were willing to believe the Communists would help them. The Nationals and Communists were so busy fighting each other they almost ignored the Japanese who were creeping in to take over the country bit by bit. At times, no one knew who they were fighting. War Lords struggled to keep control of their peasants. Bandits took advantage of everyone. There were also many guerrilla groups operating and no one knew whose side *they* were on.

No matter which side a village was on, the others would come along and retaliate. Sometimes they tortured for information. Often they murdered. No one seemed to care what happened to the peasants and farmers. They were like pawns in a giant game of their own national chess.

Eric really knew what he must do. After all he was a missionary but it would have been easier to be *told* to go rather than be *asked*.

He prayed long and hard, leaving the final decision, as always, with the Lord. 'Complete surrender' was how he described this attitude.

That weekend he went over to Pei-Tai-Ho to tell Flo what had happened and while he was there he caught flu which meant staying longer than he'd intended. And it was during those few days that Patricia began to walk. The athlete showed up in his letter to his mother when, instead of saying the baby could take 'so many steps', he said 'she can walk two metres'! He wished Mary could see his daughters but it would be a long time before his leave was due.

134

Flo was very upset when he told her about the new posting. She knew Eric well enough to know he would feel it was *right* to take it just as surely as he felt it was *wrong* to run on a Sunday all those years before.

Back in Tientsin his friends and colleagues were annoyed when he said he would go. They felt he'd let them down by giving in to the authorities. But Flo had been right. Eric was gentle and meek – but he wasn't *weak* and he *hadn't given in*. It was simply that he felt it was the right thing to do.

The college fought to keep him there and it was actually a year and a half before he left for Siao Chang. By then his book for Sunday School teachers, *The Sermon On The Mount*, was finished and he managed to get it published before leaving Tientsin.

During the spring of that year, 1937, the North China Championships were held at the Min Yuan – the sportsground he'd helped establish, and Eric attended every day.

On the 7th May, there were forty-nine boys baptised. One was the college football captain, a boy so irritable and unruly that for once Eric almost gave up hope of him ever growing into a reasonable human being. He prayed for all his students but especially for this one. To see him taking baptism was more than he'd ever expected.

When the time came for Eric to leave Tientsin it was December, probably the worst time of the year to part from his family with Christmas almost there. He'd been at the college for thirteen years and it was a wrench to leave there too.

The journey to Siao Chang hadn't changed one bit from the time Mary took her two small sons there. But Siao Chang itself had changed a lot – some for the good but more for the worse.

What bit of modernisation had taken place over the years was of no value any more. No longer a happy, peaceful community, it was a place full of misery and fear. Visiting troops had vandalised the humble little homes and numbers of people were now living, crowded together, in the few remaining houses. Hunger and disease were with them always.

The only good Eric could see was that the women and girls no longer minced about on bound feet because the National government had outlawed the cruel practice a few years earlier.

The older inhabitants remembered James and Mary with so much affection they immediately gave Eric his father's former title; Li-Mu-Shi, meaning Pastor Liddell. And to his surprise, Eric loved being back at Siao Chang and he loved his new role far better than that of teacher. His one regret was not having Florence, Patricia and Heather with him but a bit of compensation was in being reunited with Robbie, the hospital doctor.

Nearly every village had the Japanese flag of The Rising Sun flying on top of its walls and they were all closed to strangers. Each day a different password was written on a slate and anyone arriving at the gates not knowing the password would be refused admission.

If troops were stationed in a village when Eric turned up on his bike, the villagers would be afraid to speak to him, but he showed no fear. He went into their homes and told them that people in other parts of the country – and the world – were in the same situation. This made them feel better, then he would get them singing hymns. The younger ones had been taught them by their parents but when Eric sang the hymns in *English*, everyone laughed and cheered up even more.

They hadn't much to be cheerful about though. All males

under forty-five years old had been sent off to Army School and the sounds of exploding shells and machine-guns could always be heard in the distance. But with ten thousand villages on the Great Plain, no troops from any side could be in occupation all of the time.

Due to many different dialects on the Plain, Eric hired an interpreter, Wang Feng. Peasants' transport was still by mule-cart, wheelbarrow or coolie-pole so Eric bought him a bicycle. Through Wang Feng he soon learned to recognise the signs of occupation and would avoid a particular village until a later date. Sometimes, on his return, he found burnt-out homes, men killed, women attacked and those left untouched, demented with shock and fear. Then he would try to calm them down, bringing peace and sanity back to the village.

Word had come from the National government that, to prevent the cruel Japanese from hanging them by their hair – as a form of torture – all males were to have their queues (pigtails) cut off. The queue was a source of manly pride but Eric soon persuaded them when he laughed and pointed to his own balding head, saying it didn't trouble him.

Wang Feng was always finding short cuts to keep them from the paths of bandits or guerrilla fighters. It was harder to avoid the Japanese. Eric was always being stopped and questioned. They searched his clothes, shoes, pockets and wallet. Family photographs were jeered at by the soldiers who threatened and accused Eric of all sorts of things.

His response always surprised them. He remained calm and gave that wide, disarming smile. All through life this attitude and his faith in God had kept him out of most trouble.

Off he would go again, trekking through mud, floods, freezing temperatures or scorching heat. The sun-baked loess formed deep ruts which kept throwing him from his cycle. In all the villages where he stayed, he slept on the earth floor and quite often there was no food in the house for anyone.

In August, 1938, he managed a short break at Pei-Tai-Ho with the family. It was eight months since they met and they were so happy to be together again. But the picnics, swimming and donkey rides were soon over and he was back in Siao Chang.

In early December, a number of missionaries were to hold a big baptismal service for Hsi Chi village and several others surrounding it. Then they would move on to Ch'ing Ching and Ken Chia Chuang before returning to Siao Chang for yet another Christmas away from their families.

Late on the Saturday night, heavy gunfire was heard in the distance. By Sunday breakfast a scouting plane was circling overhead. This heralded an attack so the outlying villagers didn't turn up for the baptism.

Eric was just addressing the congregation, when, with a tremendous blast, two shells exploded outside the little church. Still he continued. Then, thirty-one trucks sped through the village gates bringing soldiers to search all the buildings. The villagers were terrified and wouldn't leave the church, staying on to sing hymns.

The troops barged into the church, looked around and left to return instantly, ordering the notice-board outside to be cleaned off. Four hours later they left Hsi Chi and the people emerged from the church to see notices posted everywhere telling them not to fear. The soldiers were only searching for bandits. There had been no looting or vandalism anywhere but some homes had been damaged by shell-fire and one farmer had a small shrapnel wound. Still, everyone was too afraid to turn up for the evening service so Eric told his colleagues they may as well prepare to leave for Ch'ing Ching at dawn.

Suddenly, a sound outside alerted them. The door slowly opened and a lantern appeared followed by a blurred figure. It was the local opium addict and the last person to be seen in church. In fact, they thought he was in prison.

Because of drugs he'd lost his business and his family. He'd been arrested, tried and was sure to be sentenced to die. But during his trial, he'd prayed to God and had been acquitted.

He raced back to Hsi Chi, got a lantern from his home and headed for the church. Unaware of the terror they'd known that day, he expected a service to be going on.

He went on his knees in front of Eric who said, as he now had a congregation, he would hold the service.

By January, 1939, missionaries' lives had become very dangerous. Once Eric was summoned to cycle seven miles to Japanese HQ where he was questioned and sneered at. Even when they mocked Christianity, he just smiled and they could see they were having no effect. This earned their respect and they let him go.

Because the Japanese were always stealing it, Siao Chang hospital was running out of coal so Eric volunteered to travel the 400 miles to Tientsin to get money to buy some. He hadn't seen Flo and the girls since the summer and he was worried for their safety.

It was a nightmare journey, avoiding bandits and being stopped by Japanese. One saw his Bible and asked 'You Christian?' Eric smiled proudly and declared 'Yes, I am.'

'Ah!' said the soldier, shook him by the hand and let him go. Eric thanked God and sighed with relief.

He stayed in Tientsin for a couple of days before setting off for Tehchow Ferry to the south. To reach it he had to take a ridiculously long, criss-cross route because two parallel railway lines were held by the Japanese and the land between was in Chinese hands.

At Tehchow he bought the coal and hired a barge for the river and canal journey. Different stretches of the river were in Japanese or Chinese hands and each demanded a toll to pass through. Then bandits stole half the coal.

Further along, more bandits took the rest and all his money. Eric simply turned around and travelled all the way back to Tientsin for more money. This time he hid it in a hollowed-out loaf and advised another train passenger to do the same.

Seventy miles out of Tientsin, guerrillas had wrecked the line and a freight train so passengers had to walk miles to the next line where they waited 24 hours in the bitter cold snow for a train. A Japanese soldier tried to take Eric's compass from him but he persuaded him not to.

By the time he reached Siao Chang with the fuel, he was completely exhausted. Then he heard the hospital was out of medical supplies. After two days' rest, he set off for Tientsin again in a mule-cart to get them.

At night they reached an inn where his mother had stayed with him and Robbie thirty-five years previously. There he learned of a wounded Chinese soldier lying in an old, disused temple, eight miles away. He'd lain there for five days. No one dared go near to tend him for fear of the Japanese getting to know. They would have their homes burned and probably be killed for it.

The mule-carter had great faith in the Christian God and told Eric, if he would accompany him he would feel safe to go to the man's aid. Eric agreed and the carter went off with Eric following an hour later on a bike. The ground was frozen hard and he kept falling off.

The temple lay just one hundred yards from Huo Chi village gates. It was filthy and rat infested. The man lay on the hard, cold ground in rags that a brave villager had sneaked in under darkness.

Eric promised to return for him next day and went to spend the night in another village about three miles away.

All night he lay awake. What if he ran into Japanese troops? How could he explain about the wounded man he had with him? One wrong word and the entire village would be put in danger.

He prayed and prayed, and for guidance, he opened his Bible at a random page and read 'He that is faithful in that which is least is faithful also in much; and he that is unjust in the least is unjust also in much.'

At dawn he and the carter started out for Huo Chi. But as they neared the village gate, a figure stood, frantically waving them in. They put on a spurt and just reached safety as a military convoy passed by the mud walls and continued on its way. The cart had stopped on the edge of a deep frozen loess trench and its occupants were pitched out. From all his tumbles, Eric was black and blue.

The injured soldier was placed in the cart and they made to return to Siao Chang. Then a farmer stopped them to say another man lay near to death in Pang-Chuang, a nearby village.

Off Eric and the carter went to collect him. He lay in a dirty shed on some straw. At first, in the dim light, they couldn't see him. Then they heard a moan from a far corner. The man was one of six peasants who had been dragged from their homes, questioned and sentenced to be beheaded. The others meekly knelt down for their execution but this man refused. When his turn came, a Japanese officer slashed at his neck and he fell to the ground. After the troops left, the villagers came out to bury their dead and discovered he was still alive. His head was almost severed so they carried him to the shed and bound up his wound with rags.

He was an elderly, fat man and he wouldn't fit in the cart

so they propped him up in the shafts and Eric rode alongside on his bike to see he didn't fall out.

Planes circled above them and they could hear a column of troops moving along about a mile to their left. Discovery meant instant death but the Lord was with them.

They reached Siao Chang hospital at four in the afternoon where Robbie and Annie Buchan tended both men. Their own lives were constantly in mortal danger because they took in patients from the Chinese *and* Japanese armies.

The man from the temple lived for two days but the other man recovered.

Meanwhile, Eric had gone to Tientsin for the hospital supplies and this time there were no unpleasant incidents.

Patricia was three and a half years old. Heather was two and their father regretted missing so much of their growing years. Still, his leave was due and they were looking forward to a well earned rest in Britain.

12: Be Still My Soul

By the time their leave came around, the Japanese had control of Tientsin. They held the railways and the post office. The seven daily newspapers had been replaced by Japanese papers. These were delivered to every house in town – even though no one wanted them – and the money was collected each month. The foreign concessions were still neutral though and they produced their own papers.

Before the Japanese arrived, the city suffered from their air-raids. Afterwards they were bombed by the Chinese. If guerrilla groups attacked a railway line, hostages were taken and shot.

Whenever the Japanese scored a victory, Chinese school-children were forced to march through the city waving the flag of the Rising Sun.

The Liddells longed for a peaceful break and headed for Canada before going on to Scotland. But while they were in Toronto, war broke out between Germany and Britain. On arriving in Scotland, Eric immediately volunteered as a pilot in the RAF – the most dangerous job he could think of. To his surprise they said, at thirty-seven he was too old for flying duties and he was offered an office job instead. He decided China needed him more and declined the offer.

His mother noticed he didn't smile quite as much as he used to. But when Flo told her of his experiences and she remembered the Boxer rebellion, she understood.

She adored her little grand-daughters and they loved her.

It was Eric who felt strange. He couldn't believe how his mother had changed in the years since his father died. From sprightly middle-age she'd aged to a little, white-haired old lady.

Of course, he was expected to give talks in many places, but with the nation involved in war, demands on his time weren't too bad.

His leave lasted a year during which time they all attended Elsa McKechnie's wedding. There was a special gift for her too from China. The man who Eric had rescued turned out to be an artist and, for his convalescence, Eric found some paint, canvas and brushes. The man was so grateful to him, he painted many pictures as presents. One was of a single peony and this was given to Elsa as a wedding-present because, Eric said once in a letter to her

> Like little flower in secret bower
> Scenting the air around
> Long may you live and to others give
> The fragrance you have found.

At last the leave was over and the sad farewells were made. Eric prayed it wouldn't be the last time he saw Mary. But it would be years before his next leave and he feared she didn't have many years left.

Returning to China via Canada, they never suspected what a hazardous voyage lay ahead of them.

It was a small vessel for an Atlantic crossing. Her crew and passengers numbered only three hundred. Among the passengers were several evacuee children being forced from their war-torn land to the safety of other countries.

The ship sailed in a convoy of fifty other ships in five lines. For the first two days they would have a Royal Navy escort then they would be left on their own.

144

They'd just lost sight of the Irish coast when a torpedo hit them. Fortunately it didn't explode and from then on, all ships were ordered to zig-zag. There were obviously U-boats in the area but the sea was too rough to trace them.

The next night, the ship behind theirs was sunk. The Royal Navy escort was due to leave the following morning and no sooner was it gone when a small cargo vessel blew up and sank in two minutes. For the next twenty-four hours, everybody was on lifeboat alert until the 'all clear' went. At lunchtime another boat was hit. It didn't sink but was so badly damaged it turned back for Britain.

That afternoon, the convoy split up for safety. The ship that had sailed beside them over the past two days was sunk at 6 o'clock, another at ten past six. Nine o'clock saw one fighting a U-boat on the surface.

All the remaining ships were moving at full speed. No one went to bed but sat up in their life jackets. Nearly everyone was seasick and all the children got nasty coughs but they were very brave.

At last they reached mid Atlantic where U-boats couldn't reach and they settled down to a peaceful voyage – in foggy weather.

The passengers asked Eric to hold a thanksgiving service. He only had on a sports jacket and slacks as his other clothes were packed away but he joked that God wouldn't mind.

The children's coughs developed and eventually, measles broke out. This made them a health hazard on landing. But as they were only going to Flo's relatives, they were allowed through immigration to spend the night in the Red Cross centre. There was no bedding so they slept in their clothes.

Ten days later they set sail for China to reach Tientsin by November.

Eric went straight to Siao Chang where conditions were

worse than before. It was now a garrison with the peasants being forced out each day to dig up their crops and graveyards to build a road. It was the only time Eric felt tempted to hate.

In the spring of 1941, the Japanese were talking of sending all missionaries to internment camps. Flo was expecting another baby and Eric certainly didn't want his family living in a camp so it was decided they should return to Canada. It was May when they parted and they were heartbroken. Britain and Canada weren't yet at war with Japan so the men were able to accompany their wives as far as Kale in Japan.

The last words Eric said to Florence were 'Those who love God never meet for the last time', then he turned and walked away to get the ship back to China.

He wasn't allowed to go back to Siao Chang so he moved in with an old friend at Tientsin. They'd been together at Eltham and had taught at the Tientsin college. They took long walks together, meditating on what had gone wrong with the world. Eric wrote another book: this time for Chinese pastors, telling them what to expect from people they met and giving them a text for guidance each day.

In September, 1941, he received a cable saying he had another daughter, Maureen.

Within weeks of the New Year, 1942, the college was closed to them. Not only were they barred from teaching, they weren't allowed to hold church services. All missionaries were forced to wear arm-bands, stating their nationality.

To get around the ban on church services, Eric suggested that the wives who were still there should invite friends to tea every Sunday. With enough people meeting in different houses, they could hold their services and the Japanese would never know.

When he and his friend were turned out of their flat Eric was taken in by a missionary family who had teenage children. This suited Eric. He taught them to play tennis. They all played cricket and he helped the girls to start a stamp collection like his own.

In gratitude for their hospitality, he got up at five every morning and went to queue for bread before spending his 'quiet time' with the Lord. One night there was a terrible dust storm and the man's wife was just too exhausted to clean up before going to bed. When she walked down the next morning at 6 o'clock, everywhere was spotless. Her guest had stayed up all night sweeping and dusting for her.

In the few letters from home, he learned that Heather was going to church with grannie McKenzie and that Patricia was helping her mother to bring up baby Maureen. Eric was beginning to wonder if he would ever see his new daughter – or any of his family again.

Then, in August, the unbelievable happened. Everyone was asked if they wanted to go home. Eric would have stayed but when he knew all the others were going he decided to go with them. He would get a mission posting in Canada and be with his family at last. He knew it would take time for the evacuation to get under way but he was happy. When 1943 came in he was sure it would be a matter of weeks before they left.

Britain and America had been at war with Japan for two years at that time after the Japanese attacked Pearl Harbour, but Christian missionaries had been treated almost as neutral. Then suddenly, everything changed.

At lunchtime on March 12th, 1943, word came that all British and American enemies were to report at Weihsien internment camp, hundreds of miles from Tientsin. They were to leave in three parties on three consecutive days and Eric was appointed captain of his group which would leave on March 30th. They were allowed to send four pieces of luggage on ahead and carry two suitcases with them.

At 7.30 pm on the day they left, all the Chinese lined the streets to watch the enemies being marched to the railway station. Their faces showed sympathy but no one uttered a sound or waved for fear of the troops. At midnight the filthy train set off from the station. It was packed and everyone had to sit rigid throughout the night. Next morning they changed trains at Tainan and arrived at Weihsien in the evening.

They were all tired, dirty, hungry and worried about their fate. But the inmates already there seemed happy enough and cheered the newcomers. To receive their instructions, they were lined up on the sports ground before being taken to their quarters.

In a country the size of China, Japan couldn't spare military personnel so the camp commander was really a civil servant and his armed guards were policemen.

High walls and electrified fences surrounded the camp and on top of the walls were powerful searchlights.

The camp commander encouraged the internees to form groups and committees to rule themselves in discipline, education and employment. Families were kept together while unattached males and females were housed in separate blocks. There was a hospital – with hardly any equipment – and food was very scarce. This caused hardship for the wealthy internees who were used to eating only the best. But ironically, with a meagre vegetable diet, some of them improved in health. These people suffered the most in another way. They were used to having servants; now they had to do everything for themselves.

Eric was appointed maths teacher to the children and he orgnised all the sport. Internees were expected to do three hours work each day but, within a week, Eric was already way over this limit. He volunteered to take evening classes for adults; took on the post of warden for his own block and the one next door; arranged for all the supplies for both blocks, from food to exercise books. As if this wasn't enough, he conducted the religious services too.

Everyone loved him, particularly the young ones. He went around like the Pied Piper and was known as 'Uncle Eric'. All the teachers in the camp decided to set extremely stiff exams for the sixth formers, hoping the results would get them into university when the war ended. But there was no blackboard, no chalk, very little paper and no laboratory equipment. To get over this Eric spent hours carefully *drawing* every piece of scientific equipment the students would have found in a laboratory. He detailed them so well that the pupils were able to use the apparatus when they saw it in later years.

No one seemed to notice how much Eric was doing for everybody. He was just left to get on with it. Visiting the sick, chopping wood, carrying coal, shopping for the elderly at the canteen.

The Red Cross helped enormously by supplying eggs, peanut oil, honey, candy, toothpaste, shoe-polish, Chinese cloth shoes and clogs.

Easter time saw the neutral Swiss giving each child two eggs and a pound of honey. Sometimes the goods were looted in transit and it could be weeks before more arrived.

A while after Eric went to the camp, his old friend, Annie Buchan arrived. When the Siao Chang missionaries were sent home, she was allowed to stay on at the hospital to nurse a dying patient. Later, the entire village was destroyed and Annie was sent to Weihsien.

What a shock she had when she saw that the thin, bowed figure walking towards her was Eric. He was sun-tanned and when he saw her, he gave that well known grin but he'd changed so much. To hide her shock, Annie teased him about his highly coloured shirt. 'It's made out of Flo's living-room curtains,' he said.

She soon discovered that most of the inmates were dressed in old curtains.

Naturally, with so many people crammed together in prison-like conditions, quarrels were always breaking out. Nerves were on edge and tempers easily exploded. Then Eric would step in as peacemaker. He would remember some funny tale that fitted the situation and soon had the argument solved and those involved laughing.

He was coaching hockey, tennis, volley-ball, rounders and football, often refereeing as well. He spent winter evenings repairing hockey sticks, bats and rackets with strips of old curtains, sheets and towels in readiness for the spring and summer. He was now in his early forties but once more he donned vest and shirt to run round the perimeter walls, encouraging and training the young athletes.

Annie was always asking people to stop expecting so much from him but they always pointed out, it was Eric who *volunteered* to do it.

There was one thing he refused to do and that was to take part in Sunday sport; until the day a hockey match ended in a fight. Rather than see the children behaving like that, he went out and acted as referee.

He never gave up hope for the future and never lost faith in the Lord. Before seven o'clock roll call each morning, he would be up, reading the Bible under a dim lamp fuelled by peanut oil and then he would discuss his plans for the day with God.

Annie often came across him gazing at photographs of Flo and the children. But he would put on a brave smile and replace them in his wallet then get on with some job or other.

Letters to and from home were few. The Red Cross

supplied their own special letter form which was approved by the enemy officials. It was a single sheet which held few words but this was better than having no communication at all. One day, some mail arrived and Annie watched Eric reading his. When he'd finished he bent forward and put his head in his hands. He'd never looked so dejected as in that moment and she went over to him. This time, he didn't even try to brighten up.

'I've got a splitting headache,' he told her.

Annie had been awfully concerned for him for a long time. He looked so weary and bowed. She persuaded him to walk over to the hospital with her where they diagnosed flu and sinusitis. It was January, 1945, just a week after his forty-third birthday and the hospital doctors told him he was doing far too much for his age. He must slow down a bit. Eric promised he would.

After a few days' rest, he was working again – but not quite as hard and Annie suspected it was because he was unable to. He was always plagued with severe headaches now but he laughed and said it was the camp diet that caused them.

He began lying in his room with cloths over his eyes to keep out the light and he told Annie he saw no future ahead of him; everything seemed blank. Everyone in the camp began to worry over Uncle Eric's health but when they went to visit him, he tried to cheer *them* up.

The weather was dreadfully cold and he could never stop shivering. Then, one Sunday in February, he felt a numbness down his side. Again he was taken to hospital and they said he'd had a slight stroke. But the doctors were beginning to realise there was something much more serious wrong with him than flu, sinusitis, exhaustion or even the stroke. But they had no proper equipment to make a full examination.

Annie was so distressed to see her old friend in that condition. She knew he was too intelligent a man not to realise it himself but he never spoke of it. He suffered agonising pains in his head but still managed to tease one of his young visitors who was shortly getting married. Would she be wearing old curtains for a wedding dress? he asked. He told her he'd had a nervous breakdown but by then, everyone knew, Eric had a brain tumour.

After a few days he was let out of hospital to post a letter to Florence. Only twenty-five words were allowed but he managed to say he'd been overworking; was giving up teaching and sport to take up *more physical work* like baking in the kitchens.

On the way back from the postbox he decided to call on some friends. They lived four floors up in their block and he struggled up the stairs. They gave him tea which he ate and enjoyed but they noticed his speech was slower than usual and rather slurred. A week later he went again and felt much better. The climb up the stairs had been easier and he talked more, staying much later than he'd intended. Some fresh supplies had just arrived in camp and his friend's wife scraped some ingredients together to make his favourite cake and sent it to him the next day.

That afternoon he returned the dish she'd sent the cake on and again he said he felt much better.

Snow lay deep on the ground and as he was returning to the hospital, one of the internees saw him half stumble and lean against the wall before walking on. At the hospital he got into bed then a little girl came to see 'Uncle Eric'. He chatted and made her laugh but suddenly he was gripped by a terrible pain and began to choke and cough. The girl ran for the doctor and Eric was put in a little side ward where it was quiet. When Annie heard of this she raced to see him and cradled his head in her arms.

'Annie,' he said, 'it's complete surrender.'

He began to cough again, then he lapsed into a coma. Within minutes he was dead and the whole camp fell into mourning.

There were eighteen hundred people in the camp and everyone – even non-Christians – attended his funeral in the little cemetery at Weihsien camp. Children formed a guard of honour for their much-loved Uncle Eric and his nearest friends were bearers. Wreaths came from every section of the camp and even the men were in tears as they sang 'I Know That My Redeemer Liveth'.

At the service in the freezing, wind-blown graveyard, people were surprised when his Olympic victory was mentioned. Some knew but most had no idea. Even those who'd heard of the famous Eric Liddell had no idea this was the man in Weihsien camp. It was the Reverend Cullen who conducted the service. He had been with Eric at Eltham, at the College in Tientsin and they'd shared a flat when Flo and the children left China. He felt greatly honoured to be present at the very end.

No one else could have known what Eric had told him many years before. At his funeral, he'd said, there was nothing he would want more than to have his favourite hymn sung, 'Be Still My Soul'. As they began to sing it, Annie remembered, shortly before he died, Eric had managed to scrawl on a piece of paper those very words. Be Still My Soul.

The war-torn world had only a few more weeks to go before peace returned. There had been much death and destruction everywhere and yet, when the world learned of Eric Liddell's death, it was stunned.

Memorial services were held at every single sports meeting; every religious meeting of all denominations; in schools, colleges and universities; in every town, city and village.

At the church in Dundas Street, Glasgow, where his father, James had been ordained, his entire family gathered for a service.

These services and dedications at sports meetings were still going on a year after his death. Eltham college had an extension built and called it Liddell House.

A Religious Training Centre was built in 1961 and called one of its rooms the Eric Liddell Room.

Boys' Clubs bore his name. Benefit matches and trust funds were organised for the education of his three daughters.

Scout Patrols and orphanages in China were given his name as was a boys' comic strip cartoon, relating all the athlete's exploits.

To this day, books are still being written about him. The film *Chariots of Fire* portrays him. An American film company has bought the rights to produce another film of his life.

Quite often, in church services or Sunday Schools the name, Eric Liddell, is brought up as an example of all that is good and wholesome in this world. Could any better example ever be given?

THE SACRED DIARY OF ADRIAN PLASS AGED 37¾

Illustrated by Dan Donovan

Adrian Plass

A full-length, slide-splitting paperback based on the hilarious diary entries in Christian Family magazine of Adrian Plass, 'an amiable but somewhat inept Christian'. By his own confession, Adrian 'makes many mistakes and is easily confused', but a reasssuring sense of belonging to the family of God is the solid, underlying theme. Best-selling Christian book of 1987. £2.50

THE THEATRICAL TAPES OF LEONARD THYNN

Adrian Plass

The final volume of Adrian Plass's Christian trilogy. All the familiar characters from the Sacred Diary of Adrian Plass and The Horizontal Epistles of Andromeda Veal are taking part in recording sessions to produce Leonard Thynn's extraordinary theatrical tapes. They produce a dramatic version of 'Daniel in the Lion's Den' which of course you will never be able to read in the same way again. £2.99

THE HORIZONTAL EPISTLES OF ANDROMEDA VEAL

Illustrated by Dan Donovan

Adrian Plass

Adrian Plass – diary-writer *sans pareil* – returns! This time he finds much to amuse him in the letters of Andromeda Veal, precocious eleven-year-old daughter of a Greenham woman. During a stay in hospital, Andromeda reveals herself as a shrewd commentator on her local church and the wider world, and seizes her chance to write all those letters that had to wait before – to, 'Gorgeous Chops', 'Ray Gun', 'Rabbit' Runcie, the Pope, and even Cliff Richard. £2.50